I0571429

Bright Minds, Creative Paths

Visual Learning Strategies for Neurodivergent Homeschoolers

By: Sarah Evans

Dedicated to Ian who perfects the art of happiness and spreading joy

Table of Contents

Foreword

As an accidental homeschooling family of two neurodiverse learners, I want to thank you for embarking on this journey with your child. Our journey into homeschooling began unexpectedly, born out of the realization that traditional educational environments weren't meeting our children's unique needs. What started as a daunting challenge has transformed into a deeply rewarding experience filled with growth, creativity, and connection.

Through trial and error, we've discovered that learning can be as diverse and individualized as the learners themselves. Homeschooling has allowed us to embrace our children's strengths, cater to their unique ways of processing the world, and foster an environment where they can truly thrive.

I know the path ahead may seem uncertain at times, but I encourage you to trust in your ability to guide and support your child. This book is a compilation of the insights, strategies, and tools that have helped us navigate this journey, and I hope it serves as a valuable resource for you.

May your homeschooling experience be filled with joy, growth, and discovery. Every step you take with your child is a step toward unlocking their potential and nurturing a love of learning that will last a lifetime.

CHAPTER ONE

Starting the Journey

INTRODUCTION

Disabilities are not barriers to success; rather, it is society's beliefs, the lack of accommodations, and the rigid expectations that constrain potential. Success should not be confined to outdated standards and one-size-fits-all methods. It's time to rewrite that narrative.

Embarking on the journey of homeschooling a neurodivergent child can be both exciting and daunting. You may have found, as our family did, that traditional schooling options were not a great fit for your child, or you may be curious about what you can do at home to extend what your child is learning at their brick-and-mortar school. Specialized private schools can be expensive or may require a move, which might not be suitable for your needs. This book sets out to help build your confidence as you start your homeschooling or extension schooling journey.

I aim to empower you with tips, techniques, and guides for incorporating appropriate material for your learner in a way that truly helps them grasp the concepts. I have successfully brought one neurodiverse child from elementary through high school and currently homeschool my 15-year-old, a Level 2 autistic with sensory processing disorder, a speech processing delay, and severe ADHD. Daunting? With traditional school approaches, you bet! However, with the right mix of interest-driven approaches, you will gain the confidence to explore topics that can expand your child's understanding of the world, improve communication, and incorporate sensory regulation and pacing needs.

You might feel a mix of uncertainty and hope as you consider the best ways to support your child's unique learning needs. By the end of this guide, you will build the start of a solid foundation, understanding how to adapt your homeschool and why homeschooling can be a powerful and rewarding choice for your neurodivergent learner.

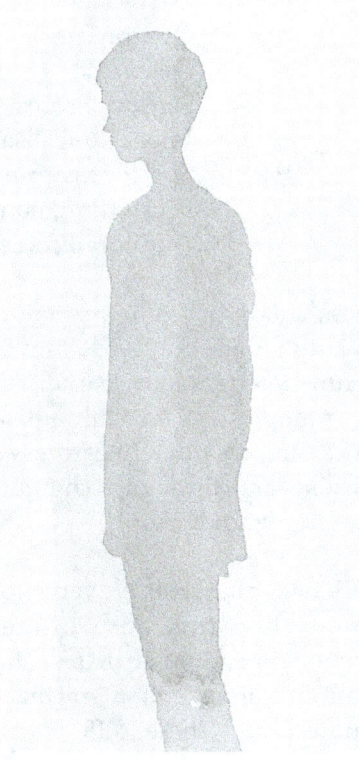

WHAT IS NEURODIVERGENCE?

Neurodivergence refers to the diverse ways in which brains function and process information. This includes a variety of neurological conditions such as autism, ADHD, dyslexia, and more. Neurodivergent individuals often have unique strengths and challenges that differ from the neurotypical population.

Neurodivergent is an umbrella term that includes a variety of neurological and developmental conditions. Some of the diagnoses that fall under neurodivergence include:

1. Autism Spectrum Disorder (ASD)
2. Attention Deficit Hyperactivity Disorder (ADHD)
3. Dyslexia
4. Dyscalculia
5. Dysgraphia
6. Dyspraxia
7. Sensory Processing Disorder (SPD)
8. Intellectual Disabilities
9. Specific Learning Disabilities (SLD)
10. Social (Pragmatic) Communication Disorder
11. Auditory Processing Disorder

These conditions can vary widely in their manifestations and impact on individuals, but they all involve atypical neurological development or functioning. Many learners may have co-morbidities meaning that, for example, a child with autism may also have ADHD and sensory processing disorder. Regardless of their labels, every child is capable of learning and through techniques presented in this book, the hope is that they learn with joy.

Understanding neurodivergence is crucial for creating an effective homeschooling environment. We already recognize that neurodivergent children have different ways of learning, communicating, and interacting with the world than their neurotypical counterparts. These differences should not be seen as deficits but variations that will respond to a tailored educational approach. By appreciating and adapting to these differences, you can better support your child's educational journey.

THE BENEFITS OF HOMESCHOOLING NEURODIVERGENT CHILDREN

Homeschooling offers a level of flexibility and personalization that traditional schooling often cannot, making it particularly beneficial for neurodivergent children. By providing a tailored and supportive learning environment, homeschooling can help unlock your child's full potential in ways that a conventional classroom may struggle to achieve. Here are some key benefits of homeschooling for neurodivergent children:

- **Individualized Learning**: One of the greatest advantages of homeschooling is the ability to tailor the curriculum to suit your child's specific needs, interests, and pace of learning. This individualized approach allows you to focus on what works best for your child, whether that's through visual learning techniques, hands-on experiments, or incorporating their special interests into the curriculum. For instance, if your child has a passion for trains, you can design lessons that incorporate train-related themes across subjects like math, science, and history. This not only makes learning more engaging but also helps your child connect new information to their existing knowledge base, reinforcing understanding and retention.

- **Flexible Schedule**: Homeschooling provides the flexibility to design a schedule that accommodates your child's unique energy levels, attention span, and daily rhythms. This can make learning more effective and less stressful, as you can plan lessons for the times of day when your child is most focused and engaged. Additionally, homeschooling allows for breaks and activities tailored to your child's needs, such as sensory breaks, which are crucial for maintaining concentration and reducing anxiety. You can also adjust the pace of learning, spending more time on challenging subjects and moving quickly through areas where your child excels.

- **Safe Learning Environment**: For many neurodivergent children, a familiar and controlled environment is essential for reducing anxiety and sensory overload. Homeschooling allows you to create a learning space that is specifically designed to meet your child's sensory needs, whether that means having a quiet, clutter-free area, using specific lighting, or incorporating sensory tools that help them focus. This safe and nurturing environment can significantly enhance your child's ability to concentrate and engage with the material, leading to more successful learning outcomes.

- **Focus on Strengths**: Homeschooling gives you the freedom to build on your child's strengths and passions, fostering a love of learning and boosting their confidence. Unlike traditional schooling, which often focuses on a standardized curriculum, homeschooling allows you to emphasize the subjects and activities that your child is most passionate about. This not only makes learning more enjoyable but also empowers your child to take ownership of their education. By focusing on their strengths, you can help your child develop a positive self-image and a strong sense of competence, which are crucial for long-term success.

- **Family Bonding**: Spending more time together through homeschooling can strengthen family bonds and provide a supportive, nurturing atmosphere for your child. This close-knit environment allows you to be more attuned to your child's needs, enabling you to provide immediate support and encouragement when challenges arise. Additionally, homeschooling often involves collaborative learning experiences, where parents and siblings participate in projects, field trips, and discussions together. These shared experiences not only enrich your child's education but also foster a deep sense of connection and belonging within the family unit.

You know your child best. You know what motivates them, what makes them giggle with glee, and what their buttons are. Imagine pouring all of the time previously spent on daily phone calls from the school, crafting IEPs, monitoring progress, communicating to different teachers and support staff how to best reach your child into crafting an effective, nurturing and successful educational environment for your learner to thrive in.

6

THE CHALLENGES OF HOMESCHOOLING

While homeschooling has many benefits, it also comes with its own set of challenges, many of which we address in the following chapters:

1. **Time and Commitment**: Homeschooling requires a significant investment of time and energy. I feel this is especially true with a neurodivergent learner. They may require one-on-one instruction, constant redirection, and daily structure that all require more time and energy than a neurotypical learner would.

3. **Resource Availability**: Finding the right resources and materials tailored to your child's needs can be challenging. It may take time to discover what works best. We will walk through ready to use resources as well as techniques for adapting existing resources to best fit your learner's needs. By challenging some of the traditional instructional methods, we will foster your confidence that even when your school doesn't look like what other's may expect, you know that your learner is getting a an excellent education focused on developing critical thinking and deeper understanding through the use of visual tools, hands-on-manipulatives, and games from elementary through high school.

4. **Socialization**: Ensuring your child has opportunities to interact with peers and develop social skills is essential. Seeking out community groups and activities can break up a week and create some fantastic opportunities for your learner to develop great friendships and community interaction. Even a simple outing to a grocery store can incorporate life skills you may be working on like finding ingredients for a recipe or social greetings. Additional resources should be found for you, the guide, as respite and community is essential for you as well. Search for local special-needs parents meetups on social media, ask your local librarian or community activity centers if they have homeschool options or create your own groups as your needs evolve.

5. **Educational Expertise**: You may feel uncertain about your ability to teach certain subjects, especially as your child progresses to higher grades. However, there are many

resources and support systems available to help you. By the end of this book, my hope is that you will feel empowered and will have sparked some creative energy and the momentum you need to take your learner's journey from reticent to self-motivated and even asking for more.

PERSONAL STORIES: FROM UNCERTAINTY TO CONFIDENCE

Many parents have successfully navigated the homeschooling journey with their neurodivergent children.

Anne's Story:

Anne was initially overwhelmed by the prospect of homeschooling her neurodivergent son, Thomas. The decision to pull Thomas from traditional pubic school at 4th grade was due to the lack of interest in educational topics and low motivation to learn. While Anne knew that this decision was best for Thomas, she worried about her ability to meet his educational needs. However, through trial and error, Anne discovered that Thomas thrived with an interest-led project based approach. By allowing the exploration of topics that were of particular interest to him, topics that were previously considered a chore were projects of choice and they both enjoyed learning together, incidentally incorporating writing, history, and life skills without making a single lesson plan. Thomas enjoyed talking about his projects to others and the passion he had for those topics showed in later applications for college. The interest-led approach allowed Thomas to heal from the public school issues that had crushed his self-confidence and the level of learning he was able to do with Anne's guidance was much deeper than surface level. He is able to speak on those same topics years later. There is a difference in the quality of learning you have when you are truly interested in knowing more.

David's Story:

David's daughter, Emma is autistic and has ADHD. She struggled in a traditional school setting with both the pace and the social stressors. The constant distractions and rigid schedule not only made it difficult for her to focus but her anxiety levels were becoming extreme. David

8

decided to homeschool Emma, allowing her to learn in a more flexible and supportive environment. He incorporated short, engaging lessons and frequent breaks. By allowing Emma to work at her pace and be being responsive to her sensory needs, Emma's academic performance improved, and she developed a love for subjects she previously found challenging.

My story:

My own son was also in public school. With several diagnoses like ASD, ADHD, sensory processing disorder and a severe speech delay, it seemed we were spending more time responding to behavior calls from the school and finding ways to force fit him to conform to the school's way of doing specific things at a specific time in a specific way. The result was "behaviors" that were developing were distressing for him, his instructional staff and the entire family. These "behaviors" were his non-verbal way of communicating his extreme distress and anxiety. At home we could see his bright curiosity and intelligence while reports from school showed aggression, refusal, elopement, very low academic scores and indications that he was severely delayed and behind his peers. After a few years of this ARD/IEP / intervention cycle, the school wanted to move him into a special needs classroom full-time. As he wasn't responding well to the instructional techniques, they also signaled they would transition him away from an academic track and focus more on functional life skills. It was exhausting to manage the constant strain we were feeling from the school and the strain the behaviors were having on our child which sometimes escalated once he was home. It was clear he was not thriving. I decided to take the energy I was spending on the daily phone calls and ARD meetings and IEP planning and find the happy child I knew he truly was. With a low-verbal child, the traditional materials marketed for homeschoolers wasn't a good fit as they required either developed speech or small motor skills for writing that caused frustration. By focusing on an adapted Montessori approach, visual schedules, and lots of sensory breaks, we found an early rhythm and approach that best fit his needs. By being able to demonstrate his understanding of more advanced concepts, it was clear that the issue wasn't him but with his prior environment. Over time, my confidence grew along with his and we transitioned to more complex subjects. Today, we celebrate his unique way of learning and he is showing his capabilities by conquering mathematics and science at the same level as his same-age peers.

EMBRACING THE JOURNEY

As you begin this homeschooling journey with your neurodivergent child, remember that it's okay to feel unsure and make mistakes. Every child is unique, and what works for one may not work for another. The key is to remain patient, flexible, and open to learning alongside your child.

In the following chapters, we will delve deeper into specific strategies and techniques for teaching math, science, and reading through visual learning. You'll find practical tips, real-life examples, resources and plenty of encouragement to help you along the way.

Homeschooling your neurodivergent child is a journey of discovery for both of you. With understanding, support, and the right tools, you can create a learning environment where your child can thrive and where you can grow in confidence as their guide.

PART ONE

BUILDING THE FOUNDATION

CHAPTER TWO

Understanding Neurodivergence

INTRODUCTION

One of the most profound challenges and joys of homeschooling a neurodivergent child is understanding their unique way of processing the world. This chapter delves into the neurological benefits of visual learning and addresses the critical distinction between communication and understanding. By embracing these concepts, you can create a more effective and supportive educational environment for your child.

Neurodivergent conditions can affect a child's response to traditional public school learning methods in various ways. Here are some examples of how specific conditions might impact a child's experience in a traditional educational setting that we will work to address and eliminate from impact your learner's true progress as you guide them through their homeschool journey:

Autism Spectrum Disorder (ASD)
Children with Autism Spectrum Disorder (ASD) often face significant challenges in sensory processing, social interactions, and cognitive flexibility. Sensory overload is a common issue, where bright lights, loud noises, and crowded classrooms can become overwhelming and lead to distress. Socially, children with ASD may struggle to understand social cues, making typical social interactions challenging and sometimes isolating. Additionally, rigid thinking can make it difficult for them to adapt to changes in routine or cope with

unexpected events, leading to anxiety and frustration.

Attention Deficit Hyperactivity Disorder (ADHD)

Attention Deficit Hyperactivity Disorder (ADHD) is characterized by difficulties in maintaining focus, regulating behavior, and controlling impulses. Children with ADHD often struggle with inattention, finding it hard to focus on tasks or follow instructions for extended periods. Hyperactivity is another hallmark, with children finding it nearly impossible to stay still, leading to frequent movement or talking out of turn, which can be disruptive in a classroom setting. Impulsivity is also common, where actions are taken without forethought, potentially causing disruptions and challenges in learning environments.

Dyslexia

Dyslexia primarily affects reading and language processing, leading to a range of learning challenges. Children with dyslexia often face difficulties in decoding words, reading fluently, and comprehending text. Spelling can be particularly problematic, as these children struggle to recognize and apply the rules of spelling, resulting in incoherent or inconsistent writing. Additionally, dyslexia often involves slow processing, where children take longer to interpret and understand written information, which can impact their overall academic performance.

Dyscalculia

Dyscalculia is a learning disability that affects a child's ability to understand numbers and mathematical concepts. Children with dyscalculia often struggle with basic math skills, including calculations and number recognition. They may also have visual-spatial problems, making it difficult to understand spatial relationships or visualize mathematical problems, which can affect tasks like geometry or map reading. Time management is another area of difficulty, as children with dyscalculia may struggle to understand and manage time-related tasks, which can impact daily routines and academic tasks.

Dysgraphia

Dysgraphia affects writing abilities, making tasks that require fine motor skills particularly challenging. Children with dysgraphia often have poor handwriting, with difficulties in letter formation that result in illegible text. Organizing thoughts and structuring written work can also be a significant challenge, as these children struggle with organizational problems that affect their ability to convey ideas coherently on paper. Additionally, fine motor skills issues can extend beyond writing, affecting other activities like drawing or using tools, which require precise hand movements.

Dyspraxia

Dyspraxia is a neurological disorder that impacts motor coordination, affecting both gross and fine motor skills. Children with dyspraxia may have difficulty with tasks that require physical coordination, such as handwriting or participating in sports. Spatial awareness is another challenge, as they may struggle to understand spatial relationships, making navigation and understanding of physical space difficult. Moreover, sequencing tasks—where multiple steps must be followed in a particular order—can be particularly challenging, leading to difficulties in following instructions or completing tasks independently.

Sensory Processing Disorder (SPD)

Sensory Processing Disorder (SPD) involves difficulties in processing sensory information, which can result in either heightened or diminished responses to stimuli. Children with SPD may be overly sensitive to noise, textures, lights, or other sensory inputs, leading to sensory sensitivities that can cause meltdowns or withdrawal in response to overwhelming stimuli. These sensory challenges can make it difficult for children to focus in environments with distracting sensory input, impacting their ability to engage in learning activities.

Intellectual Disabilities

Intellectual disabilities involve significant limitations in cognitive functioning and adaptive behavior, which affect a child's ability to learn and perform daily activities. Children with intellectual disabilities often learn at a slower pace, requiring more time to acquire new skills and concepts. Because of this, they may need an adapted curriculum that uses modified instructional materials and teaching methods tailored to their specific learning needs. Additionally, their education may need to include a focus on practical life skills, helping them develop the abilities necessary for daily living and independence.

* * *

Specific Learning Disabilities (SLD)

Specific Learning Disabilities (SLD) refer to a range of disorders that impact a child's ability to learn in specific academic areas, such as reading, writing, or math. Children with SLD may exhibit subject-specific struggles, where they face challenges in one particular area while performing well in others. This variability in performance can lead to frustration and low self-esteem, as these children may struggle to understand why they excel in some subjects but not others. The inconsistency in academic achievement often requires targeted interventions to help them succeed in their areas of difficulty.

Social (Pragmatic) Communication Disorder

Social (Pragmatic) Communication Disorder affects a child's ability to use language effectively in social contexts. Children with this disorder may have significant communication challenges, finding it difficult to use verbal and nonverbal communication appropriately in social interactions. These difficulties often extend to the classroom, where they may struggle to participate in group work, follow classroom norms, or engage in typical social interactions with peers. This can lead to isolation and challenges in building relationships within the school environment.

Auditory Processing Disorder

Auditory Processing Disorder (APD) impacts how the brain processes auditory information, making it difficult for children to interpret and understand sounds, especially in noisy environments. Children with APD often have listening difficulties, which can make it challenging to follow verbal instructions or participate in discussions. This disorder can also lead to delays in language development and comprehension, affecting their ability to engage fully in the learning process and communicate effectively with others.

Understanding these diverse impacts can help tailor your homeschooling approach to better meet the unique needs of your neurodivergent learner, creating a more effective and supportive learning environment. By acknowledging where your learner may struggle, you can adapt the environment, learning materials and even learning method to open your learner's educational world.

* * *

THE NEUROLOGICAL BENEFITS OF VISUAL LEARNING

Visual learning leverages the brain's ability to process images faster and more efficiently than text. For neurodivergent children, this approach can be especially beneficial.

1. **Enhanced Retention**: Visual aids like diagrams, charts, and pictures help in better retention of information. Neurodivergent learners often find it easier to remember visual data compared to auditory or textual information.

2. **Simplified Complex Concepts:** Visual learning breaks down complex concepts into more digestible parts. For example, a visual representation of a math problem can make it easier to understand and solve. Hands-on-manipulatives can also help to deepen understanding especially for minds that organize concepts visually. Arabic numeral representation of mathematics doesn't address numerical concepts. Using number blocks, counters, tiles or other visual aids can cement a concept with a higher level of understanding than methods relying only penciling Arabic numerals on paper.

3. **Increased Engagement:** Visual tools can make learning more engaging and enjoyable. Interactive visuals, such as educational videos and animations, capture the learner's interest and keep them focused. When it feels more like a game or like play, you naturally have increased focus and engagement.

4. **Support for Non-Verbal Learners:** For learners who struggle with verbal communication, visual learning provides an alternative means to express understanding and knowledge. When I incorporated Montessori style learning with my learner during his early learning days, he found it easier to demonstrate knowledge of concepts without relying on verbal response.

COMMUNICATION VS. UNDERSTANDING

A common misconception others have of our children is that any difficulty in communication equates to a lack of understanding. This is far from the truth. Neurodivergent children may have different ways of expressing themselves or different methods of taking in and retaining information, but this does not mean they do not grasp the concepts being taught. By meeting your learner where they are, you allow them to express their true capability. As understanding grows, communication improves in whichever way they choose to communicate. As communication flows, anxiety and frustration, along with their accompanying behaviors, will diminish.

One of the most important principles to adopt as a parent-educator is to always assume competence. This means believing in your child's ability to understand, learn, and engage, even when their communication style differs from what is typically expected. Narrating tasks as you do them and explaining the reasons behind your choices out loud is a powerful way to provide your learner with the input and context they need, even when it feels like they are not paying attention.

I recall a time when we were working through a topic in history about the Roman Empire. We had just finished listening to some audiobooks with Percy Jackson and learned the difference between the Greek and Roman aspects of the gods. My autistic learner, Ian built a Lego version of a small Roman village and included a Roman temple to match up to part of the story we had listened to. I thought I might be able to expand on this and found some materials on architectural structures of the temples in ancient Rome but verbal communication was a significant challenge so I wasn't sure if I'd picked up on an interest or not. During our study sessions, Ian often seemed disengaged, staring off into space or focusing intently on a toy or object nearby while I pointed out different styles of columns or building techniques in a book we had borrowed from the library. I would just wonder out loud why certain materials were used or express surprise at how far materials had to travel or how many people were needed to build it. It felt like a very long one-sided conversation. When I found some short virtual tours of some of the Roman ruins that pepper Europe, he seemed to be disinterested. I worried that the concepts were not connecting, that perhaps the material was too complex or that my explanations or methods were not effective.

Despite my concerns, I continued to narrate each step of our research process. I described the significance of each building, the materials

18

used, and the cultural context behind the architectural designs. I explained why certain decisions were made by the Romans and how those decisions impacted their society. It often felt like I was talking to myself, as Ian's gaze remained averted, and there were few signs of active engagement. However, I reminded myself Ian needed time needed to process the information and when my own frustration started to turn into agitation, I decided it was best to take a break from the concept and perhaps revisit it later.

A few weeks later, we visited a local museum that had a display on the Roman Empire. As we approached a model of the Roman Colosseum, Ian suddenly became animated. Without prompting, he named the types of arches and asked how they were constructed and noted the Romans chose to build with certain materials and note others. He pointed out details in the model that I hadn't even noticed and made connections to other architectural structures we had studied. It was a moment of profound realization for me—despite the lack of visible engagement during our lessons, Ian had been absorbing the information all along. He had understood the concepts on a deep level, but his way of processing and expressing that understanding was different from what I had expected. The next summer, I gave him some options on where to do on a summer road trip for some experiential learning and the first place he picked was to go and see The Parthenon in Nashville so we made the trip and he was so excited to see the replica up close and learn about how they made casts to be as true to the original as possible.

Many neurodivergent learners, like Ian, may have difficulty maintaining eye contact while processing speech. For them, looking away is not a sign of disengagement but a strategy to focus on the verbal content without the distraction of non-verbal cues. This is especially true for those on the autism spectrum, where processing both non-verbal facial expressions and spoken words simultaneously can be overwhelming. By allowing their minds to focus solely on the auditory information, they can better grasp and retain what is being said.

As a guide for your learner it's crucial to recognize and respect these different processing styles. By meeting your learner where they are— whether that means narrating your actions, explaining concepts out loud, or giving them the space to process in their own way—you are creating an environment where true understanding can flourish. Over time, as your child's comprehension deepens, you will likely see an improvement in their communication, in whatever form that may take.

Remember, communication is not just about speaking; it's about connecting and understanding. By assuming competence and providing the right support, you allow your learner to express their knowledge and ideas in ways that make sense to them, reducing anxiety and frustration while fostering growth and confidence.

DECODING COMMUNICATION STYLES

* * *

Understanding your child's communication style is crucial. Working with a licensed speech pathologist is typical in our communities especially for those learners that struggle with verbal processing, verbal sounds or utterance and social skills.

Non-Verbal Communication: Some children may rely on gestures, facial expressions, or alternative communication devices (AAC). Developing skills in sign language or through an AAC can alleviate a lot of frustration and calm disruptive behaviors. Pay attention to non-verbal cues as they often convey a lot of information. Working with a speech pathologist can help find the best tools to work with your learner as they grow. Alternative methods such as the Rapid Prompting Method have also found some favor in our community [ref[1]].

 Echolalia: Repetition of words or phrases can be a way for children to process and understand language. It is not merely mimicry but a step towards comprehension. My own son was considered pre-verbal until he was close to 6 or 7. By parroting short phrases from his favorite movies with different vocal intonations, this version of verbal communication was showing his personality, humor, and his wants/needs.

 Delayed Response: Neurodivergent children might need more time to respond to questions or instructions. Patience is key; allow them the time they need without pressure. Breaking down tasks into smaller steps, repeating instruction and allowing time for processing is key to breaking the frustration cycle. As your learner's executive function develops, your techniques for adapting to their speech or processing delay

STRATEGIES FOR BRIDGING THE GAP

---

[1] MUKERJEE, MADHUSREE. "A Transparent Enigma." *Scientific American*, vol. 290, no. 6, 2004, pp. 49–50. *JSTOR*, http://www.jstor.org/stable/26047753. Accessed 6 Aug. 2024.

Use Visual Supports: Incorporate visual schedules, storyboards, and picture cards to aid in communication and understanding. You can use a picture based (PECS) schedule for your elementary learners. Be sure to incorporate movement breaks like neighborhood walks and include preferred actives on the schedule. Allow your learner to assist you in building this visual schedule. By having a say, they develop ownership. You may also find that incorporating small rewards for finishing their tasks within the specified block to be helpful motivation. For older learners your visual schedule may be a text based list but similar principles apply. Incorporate sensory regulation breaks to improve focus. We use a visual timer that has a colored band that gets smaller as the focus time completes. With a student that struggles with executive function, utilization of concepts like "15 minutes" or writing down times on a schedule are not typically helpful their minds process time in a different way. A visual timer provides a clearer understanding of "15 minutes" and as you use it more frequently, they will develop an internal sense of time that will help them to manage more independently for tasks as they develop.

My Daily Responsibilities

Morning

Evening

Done ✓

Early Learner Visual Schedule Support

* * *

22

M T W T F S S

today's mood:

habits:

focus on getting these done:

○ ....

○ ....

○ ....

schedule changes / appointments:

routine

morning

afternoon

evening

today's schedule:

____ : ____

____ : ____

____ : ____

____ : ____

____ : ____

____ : ____

____ : ____

____ : ____

set reminders:

chores:

brain dump:

water intake:

◊◊◊

◊◊◊

◊◊◊

Homeschool Daily Text Based Planner

Simplify Language: Use clear, simple language and repeat important points to ensure comprehension. Breaking down tasks into smaller chunks can make larger projects more approachable. For younger students, this may mean your tasks look more similar to "complete 10 addition flash cards" instead of "math". For older students, guiding them through breaking down a larger task can help them develop their own executive function skills for independent living. Setting aside time either in the morning or in the evening to prepare for the day and then reviewing that plan as you move through your day is immensely helpful both to your learner and for you as their guide. Here is a goal breakdown worksheet with a progress bar at the bottom. Many neurodivergent children experience time-blindness and difficulties with executive function. Guiding them through breaking down a larger goal or project into achievable blocks can increase their motivation for tackling it. Start small with a goal like "Clean My Room" to help orient you both to the technique. Use the bottom progress bar to color in your learner's progress as them complete each task for a visual indicator of how much progress they have made. As you become more confident, you'll find it a useful exercise to do for your homeschool tasks and perhaps even your own projects.

* * *

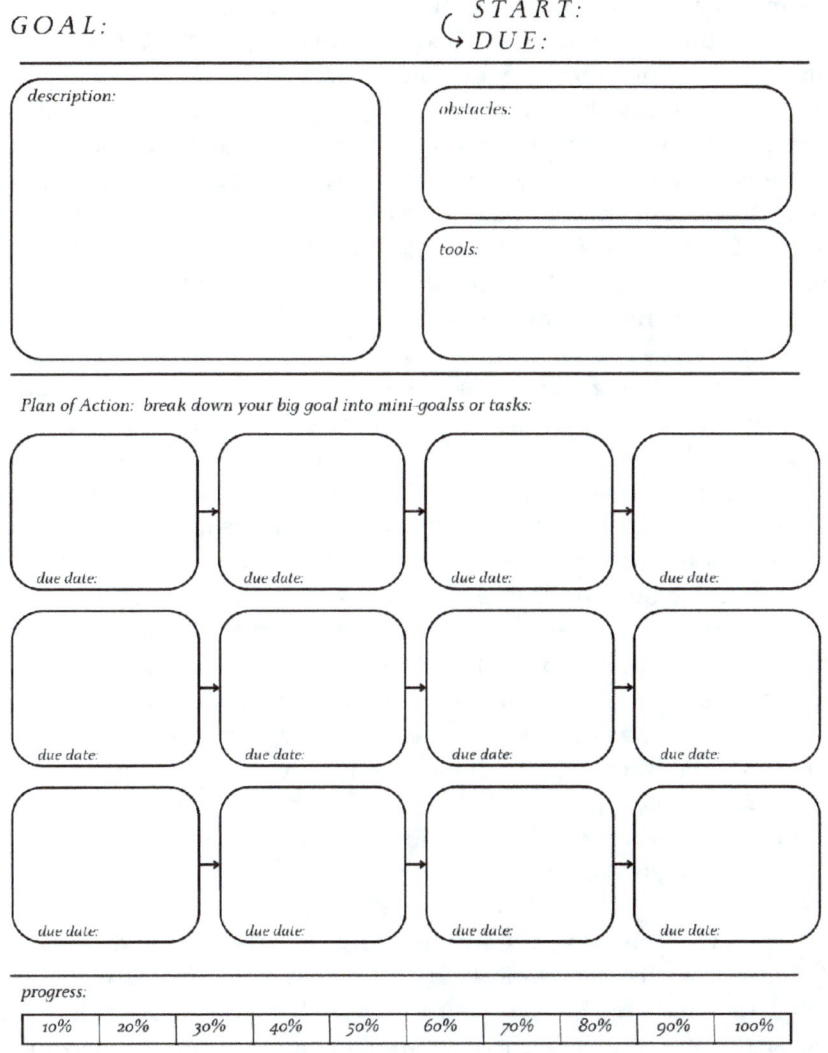

Goal Breakdown Worksheet

Encourage Alternative Expression: Allow your child to use drawings, symbols, or digital tools to express their thoughts and understanding. It can seem like your learner is not paying attention to a video or reading but by allowing them to doodle or fidget while they are listening to an audiobook, short lecture, or video, the doodling is actually helping them to organize information in their minds. Autistic learners may find that looking away from faces helps them to focus on the information instead of all of the non-verbal signals they would need to process otherwise. Before correcting such behaviors as "negative", allow them to explore their own way of soaking up information. It may be a different seating style, bouncing on their toes, facing away from a presentation or keeping a fidget or doodle pad near them while they are learning. Embrace these differences instead of trying to mold them into how it "should" look. Homeschooling is an excellent environment to encourage your learner to be exactly who they are as they come. After all, being comfortable and feeling safe are essential for learning to progress.

Use Graphic Organizers: While you are going through a topic, employ graphic organizers like Venn diagrams, flowcharts, and mind maps to help with organizing thoughts and ideas. Creating visual representations of what you are talking through can also help solidify concepts. For example, reimagining historical events in the form of simple stick-figure comics is great fun and can be collaborative between the guide and learner. It forces you to think about their lives in that time beyond the dry textbook rendition of the event. We've had great fun drawing out some of the Greek epics in stick-figure form. You don't have to be great artist to have some fun with graphical organization of the ideas. For mathematics and science, flowcharts give you time to talk through each element and recognize when there are decisions or observations that may need to be included for your neurodiverse learner that may not be explicitly understood when working through a topic.

Incorporate Technology: Leverage educational apps and software designed for visual learning. These tools can make lessons more interactive and engaging. I want to stress that over-reliance on these apps can get in the way of critical thinking and learning, so use them with your own limits There are some fantastic apps for unlocking algebraic concepts and opportunities for virtual field trips though that you really can't get through other medium. I provide a list of some of these in the final chapter.

Customize Learning Materials: Tailor your learning materials to your child's interests and strengths. Personalized visuals can make learning more relatable and effective. You can take even the driest traditional textbook and transform the information within it to a visual style that

26

will engage your particular learner. My early learner would get much more engaged with a retelling of stories using felt finger puppets than a book based sit-down. As an older learner, we use a lot of graphic novel versions of history, literature, math and science! I provide a list of some of those resources as we get more specific for each topic and also provide them in the last chapter: Resources for Visual Learning.

Incorporate Physical Activity: Take frequent movement breaks either outside or inside. If you have a treadmill or a trampoline, use them to encourage movement throughout the day. Alternative seating options like large yoga balls can both strengthen your learner's core and allow them the nervous system regulatory movement that enables organization of material they are learning in their mind. Stimming behaviors are communication as well. It may be a way for them to self-calm or to recover from a taxing situation. As long as there is no self-harm, I don't discourage healthy stimming behaviors and I let it communicate to me that either we need to do some sensory regulation or allow for a brain break before new information can be focused on. Be flexible in your timing and incorporate lots of movement to help regulate, calm, and organize the mind to be ready to take in new information.

We will work to incorporate these supports into your everyday homeschool to augment your learner's needs and adapt your instruction.

CONCLUSION

Understanding the distinction between communication and understanding is vital in homeschooling neurodivergent children. By recognizing their unique communication styles and leveraging the benefits of visual learning, you can create a more inclusive and effective educational experience. The journey may be challenging, but with patience and the right strategies, you can help your child thrive academically and personally.

In the next chapter, we will explore how to create a visual learning environment that caters to your child's needs, providing practical tips and resources to set up your homeschool for success.

CHAPTER THREE

Setting Up for Success

CREATING AN EFFECTIVE LEARNING ENVIRONMENT

Creating an effective learning environment at home is crucial for the success of your homeschooling journey, especially for neurodivergent learners. A well-designed space can enhance focus, reduce anxiety, and make learning more enjoyable. Here are some specific projects and strategies to create a customized learning space in your home:

PERSONAL STORIES: TRANSFORMING A LEARNING SPACE

Liam's Sensory-Friendly Homeschool: The Transformation of a Learning Space

Liam, a seven-year-old with sensory processing disorder, faced significant challenges in a traditional classroom setting. The constant noise, bright lights, and overwhelming stimuli made it difficult for him to focus, leading to frequent anxiety and behavioral issues. His parents noticed that despite their best efforts, Liam was struggling not just academically but emotionally, and they decided to take a different approach by homeschooling him.

However, even after transitioning to homeschooling, Liam continued to experience difficulties. They originally just used part of a playroom to sit down for school tasks with books and materials stored in the living room that they had to constantly move back and forth. The playroom was initially cluttered and visually overwhelming, with too many distractions that made it hard for him to concentrate. His parents quickly realized that in order to provide Liam with the supportive environment he needed, they had to reevaluate and redesign a dedicated learning space.

Evaluating the Learning Environment
Liam's parents began by assessing the physical environment and identifying the key factors contributing to his struggles. They noticed that the room was filled with items that weren't related to learning, creating visual clutter that distracted Liam and increased his anxiety. The lighting was also too harsh, and the space lacked a clear organizational structure that could help Liam understand what was expected of him throughout the day.

Recognizing the need for change, Liam's parents embarked on a project to create a sensory-friendly, organized learning space tailored to his needs. The first step was to declutter the room. They removed unnecessary items and introduced storage solutions like bins and shelves to keep learning materials neatly organized and out of sight when not in use. They used the shelving to create separation in the playroom so that one area was dedicated to school and included the materials needed for his current studies. This significantly reduced visual distractions, creating a cleaner, more focused environment for Liam.

Creating a Sensory-Friendly Environment
Understanding Liam's sensitivity to sensory input, his parents transformed a corner of the room into a dedicated sensory-friendly learning area. They incorporated soft lighting, using adjustable lamps with warm bulbs to create a calming atmosphere. The walls were painted in soothing colors like soft blues and greens, which helped to further reduce anxiety and promote concentration.

To address Liam's need for a quiet retreat, they set up a small tent in the corner where he could go whenever he felt overwhelmed. This space became Liam's safe haven, providing him with a quiet, enclosed area where he could take breaks and regulate his sensory input. The tent was equipped with sensory tools like stress balls, a weighted lap pad, and noise-canceling headphones, allowing Liam to self-soothe when necessary.

Implementing Visual Schedules and Organizational Tools

One of the key improvements in Liam's learning environment was the introduction of a visual schedule. His parents created a daily routine using pictures and color-coded charts, which they displayed prominently on a magnetic board. This visual timetable helped Liam understand the structure of his day, reducing the uncertainty that often triggered his anxiety. By having a clear, visual guide to follow, Liam was better able to transition between activities, which significantly improved his focus and behavior.

In addition to the visual schedule, Liam's parents incorporated other visual and organizational tools into the learning space. A small whiteboard was installed for drawing diagrams and brainstorming, which allowed Liam to visually process new concepts. They also set up an interactive wall with a magnetic alphabet board and a world map with pins, making learning both engaging and accessible. The simplicity and organization of the space helped Liam feel more in control, which in turn improved his ability to concentrate on his lessons.

The Transformation: Before and After

Before the changes were made, Liam's homeschooling experience was marked by frequent meltdowns, difficulty concentrating, and a general sense of feeling overwhelmed. The cluttered space, harsh lighting, and lack of structure contributed to his struggles, making learning a frustrating and anxiety-inducing experience.

After implementing the dedicated learning space, the transformation was remarkable. The clean, organized environment reduced distractions and allowed Liam to focus on his work without feeling overwhelmed. The sensory-friendly elements, such as the calming colors, soft lighting, and quiet retreat area, significantly decreased his anxiety levels. The visual schedule provided Liam with the structure he needed to feel secure, leading to fewer behavioral issues and a more positive attitude toward learning.

* * *

Liam's progress after the transformation was clear. He became more engaged in his lessons, his focus improved, and he started to approach learning with a sense of curiosity and excitement rather than fear and frustration. The personalized environment not only supported his sensory needs but also empowered him to take more ownership of his education. His parents were thrilled to see the positive changes in their son and knew that creating the right environment had made all the difference.

Liam's story illustrates the profound impact that a well-thought-out learning space can have on a neurodivergent child's education. By addressing sensory needs, decluttering the space, and implementing visual organizational tools, Liam's parents were able to create an environment where he could thrive, both academically and emotionally.

DESIGNING A DEDICATED LEARNING AREA

Project Idea: Setting Up a Dedicated Learning Space

Creating an effective learning environment is crucial for homeschooling success, especially for neurodivergent learners who may be sensitive to sensory input or easily distracted. Whether you have a full room to dedicate or just a corner of a shared space, here's how you can transform your home into an ideal learning space that balances comfort, organization, and focus.

Declutter and Organize

Start by decluttering the area you plan to use for learning. Remove unnecessary items and organize the space to minimize distractions. Use shelves, bins, and drawers to keep supplies tidy and easily accessible. For early learners, organizing activities in bins with pictures that match their visual schedule can help them stay focused and reduce distractions. While this requires some prep and maintenance, it allows you to include sensory bins and break activities within reach, adding flexibility to the learning process.

If space is limited, consider using a rolling cart to hold the day's supplies. This allows you to store materials neatly when not in use and easily move them into the learning space when needed. A rolling cart is especially helpful if your learning area is a shared space or a corner of another room, as it keeps everything organized and ready to go without taking up permanent space.

Calming Colors and Lighting

The environment's color scheme can significantly impact your learner's focus and mood. Opt for calming, neutral colors like soft blues, greens, or beiges to create a soothing environment. These colors can help reduce anxiety and create a sense of calm during learning sessions. If your space is part of a larger room, you can use temporary room dividers or even hang fabric to define the area and bring in those calming tones.

* * *

Good lighting is essential. Whenever possible, use natural light, which is easier on the eyes and can boost mood and energy. Add adjustable lamps with soft lighting to reduce eye strain and create a comfortable reading environment. If the learning space is a small corner, consider using clip-on lights or small desk lamps that can be positioned as needed.

Comfortable Seating

Comfortable seating is key to maintaining focus during learning activities. If you have the space, provide ergonomic chairs that support good posture. However, if your learner prefers alternative seating options—like a beanbag, floor pillows, or a soft, padded chair— incorporate those choices into your setup. For some learners, the ability to change seating positions throughout the day can help them stay engaged and reduce discomfort. Both of my learners feel really uncomfortable at a tabletop or desk situation as it limits movement and they both prefer a soft seating option. Your learner's preferences and your own may not match. I had to take a step back and not project what I thought would work best for me but observe what worked best for them.

Even in a small space, a variety of seating options can be made available. For example, floor cushions can be stored in a basket and brought out when needed, or a folding chair can be kept nearby for quick use.

Creating a Distraction-Free Zone

Reducing distractions is crucial for many neurodivergent learners. Noise control is an important aspect of this. Use noise-canceling headphones or a white noise machine to block out background noise. Thick curtains, rugs, or even wall tapestries can help absorb sound, making the learning environment quieter and more conducive to concentration.

Visual clutter can also be distracting, so keep the learning area as clean and simple as possible. Use storage solutions to maintain a tidy workspace, limiting the number of items on desks and walls. If your learner is easily distracted by wall decor, consider using removable or temporary decorations that can be covered or removed during learning sessions.

In addition, be mindful of electronic devices. Limit access to devices that are not related to learning, and use apps or tools that help manage screen time to keep the focus on educational activities. For example, I have a strict no-screen time policy until all of the school tasks are completed. My learner can take breaks with Legos, books, drawing or physical activity but seems to take much longer to get back on track if a cartoon was on or an electronic game was played as he tends to perseverate on moments that were exciting in the game and it's difficult to get his mind reset and ready to learn.

Establishing Routine and Personal Touches
Establishing a consistent daily routine and schedule is vital for providing structure and reducing unpredictability, which can be distracting for some learners. Having a clear, predictable routine helps set expectations and makes transitions between activities smoother.

While keeping the space distraction-free is important, it's also essential to allow your child to personalize their learning area. Encourage them to add their artwork, favorite colors, or motivational posters to the space. If these personal touches become too distracting during lessons, you can easily cover them up or opt for a more minimalist style while learning is in session.

Whiteboard, Chalkboard, and Interactive Walls
Incorporate tools like whiteboards or chalkboards into your learning space for writing, drawing diagrams, and visual brainstorming. These can be used to explain concepts and organize thoughts. While larger wall-mounted boards are an option, we prefer using lap-sized whiteboards for tasks like working out math problems. If you want to get creative, using a dry-erase marker on a big picture window can also be a fun way to engage your child with what you already have.

You can also dedicate a section of the wall for interactive learning activities, such as a magnetic alphabet board, a world map with pins, or a math facts wall with removable sticky notes. Tailor this interactive wall to match your learner's interests and current topics of study, allowing them to engage more deeply with the material. When my learner was younger, we used All About Spelling which came with magnetic sight words and sounds. Having a magnetic board at the ready helped with review and with focus on new sound blends.

We keep a space dedicated to celebrations of our learning and I'll post certificates of accomplishment or progress markers on goals we are working on. Part of our skill building is to work on executive function and impulse control and that includes setting and being motivated by longer term goals. Having those out as visual reminders can help develop those areas of the brain so that the skill can be generalized and used independently as an adult.

Visual Timetable and Display Boards

Visual schedules or timetables are crucial for helping neurodivergent learners understand their daily routine and tasks. Create a dedicated space for your visual schedule using pictures, icons, or color-coded charts. Templates for an example daily schedule or rhythm can be found in Chapter 2 in both visual and text formats. I like to have a sit down with my learner at the end of the day to fill out the next day's schedule sheet. We discuss any changes to our normal schedule like therapy appointments of dentist visits and reiterate the goals we are working on in scientific, math and the humanities. We then use pencil to block out our day for when we are going to be working on our different topics and include movement and brain breaks. I set up rewards for my teen right now for longer term goal setting tasks so we review those, discuss how they are doing and talk about how close they are to the reward and how far they have come towards it to keep him motivated and on track. Allow your learner to make decisions about the order of topics or the types of breaks so that they have buy-in for the day's plan. If there are outings to parks, museums, or appointments then we prepare whatever we will need for that outing the night before like packing lunches, locating paperwork, filling water bottles, and finding shoes and sunglasses to prevent snags the next day. In the morning we will review the schedule sheet and I find that the night before review and the morning reminder is enough to get him on task and following the plan. My next-day self is also very thankful for the lunch and bag prep the night before!

Additionally, use display boards like cork boards or magnetic boards to showcase visual aids, flashcards, and other educational materials. Rotating the content regularly keeps it fresh and engaging. You don't have to stay limited to your dedicated learning space for everything. For example, this year we are studying a foreign language and we use our kitchen cabinets to display language activity cards related to eating and kitchen activities. This keeps the material readily available and serves as a visual reminder to practice or incorporate the topic into mealtime conversations and kitchen chores.

By blending organization, comfort, and focus into your learning space, you can create an environment that supports your child's unique needs and helps them thrive academically. Whether you have a full room or just a corner, these tips ensure that every inch of your space is optimized for success.

SENSORY REGULATION

All learners need to have their tasks broken up into manageable pieces and many of our learners may be in need of different types sensory regulation through out their day. If you have access to an occupational therapist as part of your care team, you can work with them to create a "sensory diet" for your learner based on activities they have seen that work the best. Below, I've compiled a list of activities to create your own sensory diet that you can do throughout the day depending on whether your learner is having difficulty with focus (see organizing), reducing anxiety or frustration (see calming) or to increase energy and alertness (see alerting):

Organizing Activities
These activities help learners who need to improve focus, coordination, and body awareness.

1. Weighted Blanket or Vest: Using a weighted blanket or vest for short periods can provide deep pressure input, helping to organize sensory input.
2. Animal Walks: Encourage learners to move like different animals (e.g., bear crawl, crab walk) to engage large muscle groups and promote body awareness.
3. Wall Push-Ups: Have learners push against a wall to provide proprioceptive input, helping them feel more grounded.
4. Heavy Work: Carrying books, pushing a cart, or moving furniture can provide the organizing input that helps with focus and coordination.
5. Obstacle Course: Set up a simple obstacle course that involves crawling, jumping, and balancing to help organize movement and focus.
6. Therapy Ball Exercises: Sitting on or rolling over a therapy ball can help organize sensory input through gentle bouncing or pressure.
7. Chair Push-Ups: Encourage learners to push up on the arms of a chair, lifting their body slightly off the seat to engage their muscles.

Calming Activities
These activities help learners who need to reduce anxiety, overstimulation, or restlessness.

1. Deep Breathing Exercises: Teach learners to take slow, deep breaths to help calm their nervous system.
2. Yoga Poses: Poses like "Child's Pose" or "Tree Pose" can be calming and help with focus.
3. Gentle Rocking: Rocking in a rocking chair or sitting on a

therapy ball and gently bouncing can provide soothing vestibular input.

4. Quiet Space with Soft Lighting: Create a designated quiet area with dim lighting and soft textures where learners can retreat when overwhelmed.

5. Progressive Muscle Relaxation: Guide learners in tensing and then slowly relaxing each muscle group to reduce tension and promote calmness.

6. Listening to Soft Music: Soft, rhythmic music or nature sounds can help calm an overstimulated learner.

7. Weighted Lap Pad: Using a weighted lap pad during seated activities can provide calming deep pressure input.

Alerting Activities

These activities help learners who need to increase their energy, focus, and alertness.

1. Jumping Jacks: Performing jumping jacks can quickly increase alertness and energy levels.

2. Skipping or Hopping: Encourage learners to skip or hop in place to raise their energy and improve focus.

3. Spinning on a Swivel Chair: Controlled spinning for short periods can stimulate the vestibular system and increase alertness.

4. Chewing Crunchy Snacks: Eating crunchy snacks like carrots or apples can provide oral sensory input that helps with alertness.

5. Bouncing on a Therapy Ball: Quick, rhythmic bouncing on a therapy ball can help wake up the body and mind.

6. Quick Sprints: Running short sprints or dashing between two points can quickly boost energy and alertness.

7. Cold Water Splash: Splashing cold water on the face or drinking a cold beverage can help increase alertness.

COMMON HOUSEHOLD ITEMS FOR VISUAL LEARNING

Many household items can be repurposed to create engaging visual learning tools without spending a penny at the store. Here are some examples:

- **Mason Jars**: Use for sorting and organizing small items, like counters for math activities or letters for spelling games. I keep a small jar of coins for money counting activities and we also use them for game markers. Craft supplies in clear jars like pom-poms, Q-tips, etc make supplies easy to organize and find later. We cleared out a bookshelf for our homeschool supplies and one shelf was dedicated to my growing collection of cleaned spaghetti sauce jars that holds craft supplies, letter tiles, and math number tiles. If you are worried about glass and breakage, you can reuse up some plastic jar sized containers with screw-on lids instead.

* * *

- **Plastic Bins or shoe boxes:** Store and categorize learning materials, such as art supplies, manipulatives, and books. I prefer the clear ones so I can see what is inside but labeled shoe boxes can be used as well for a budget friendly option. I affixed adhesive velcro dots to the front of my bins and had matching PECS style labels for my early learner. This served as a visual to match their visual schedule and could be moved to a "completed" strip once the activity was done.

- **Popsicle Sticks:** Create DIY math manipulatives, craft projects, or use them as markers for reading games. You can create a catapult to investigate physics concepts with rubber bands, popsicle sticks and a bit of tape. Popsicle sticks can also be used to glue on paper figures to reenact a historical conversation. They can be used to build structures, be painted to create a sorting game or as creative bookmarks.

* * *

- **Index Cards:** Make flashcards for vocabulary, math facts, or memory games. These are great to break down a larger list into bite sized bits. As your learner gets older, the content can be adapted to their needs. You can also print and tape on small pictures as needed for additional visuals.

- **Clothespins**: Use for clip-and-count activities, attaching flashcards to a line, or creating matching games.

- **Baking Sheets:** Use as magnetic boards for letter and number magnets or create sensory trays with sand or rice for writing practice. We used one for magnetic sight words that were printed on strips and on felt figures for early learning to tell stories. You can pick up adhesive magnet strips at your local office supply and regular crafting materials to create all sorts of interactive manipulatives.

- **Egg Carton**s: Use for counting games, sorting activities, or DIY science projects like planting seeds. Take one with you on an outing to collect and sort found items like interesting rocks or leaves.

- **Cardboard**: boxes can be cut or folded and repurposed as historic forts, ramps for demonstrating kinetic energy with balls or toy cars, or they can be used as table or floor savers under art projects. You can use cardboard to craft armor worn by Roman soldiers or create mini villages from books you are reading. We currently host a 4 foot long spacecraft made from folded printer paper for walls and tape. No expensive supplies needed!

- **Mail tubes:** We use toilet paper and mail tubes to create tunnels for balls or toy cars. Increasing the angle or changing other conditions leads to different outcomes. For early learners, toilet paper tubes can be used as noise makers by adding a little rice and closing the tops and bottoms with some colorful contact paper. We've used a series of tubes with Lincoln Logs to understand how scientists think Easter Island statues were moved and the Egyptian pyramids were built.

PRACTICAL TIPS FOR PERSONALIZING THE LEARNING ENVIRONMENT

- Involve Your Child: Involve your child in setting up the learning space. Let them choose some of the decorations or organize their supplies. This can help them feel more comfortable and invested in their learning environment.
- Create a Routine: Establish a consistent routine for homeschooling. Consistency helps neurodivergent children feel secure and understand what to expect each day.
- Flexible Learning Areas: Designate different areas for different activities, such as a reading nook, a science experiment table, or a quiet corner for breaks. This allows your child to move around and choose spaces that suit their current needs and can also help with focusing. If you have the ability to have a separate space for school, this can help your learner switch into "learning mode" when they are at the science table, for example. Just like the bed is for sleeping in and the kitchen table is for eating at, a separate space for learning can keep both you the guide and your learner on track.

CONCLUSION

Setting up a visual learning environment tailored to your child's needs is a critical step in your homeschooling journey. By organizing your space effectively, incorporating essential tools and resources, and adapting the environment to meet sensory needs, you can create a supportive and stimulating learning atmosphere.

Traditional teaching methods or what is called "talk and chalk" have been proven to be less successful than tactile and visual methods of learning. Even with neurotypical learners, these traditional teaching methods have led to higher drop-out rates and a significant difference in the capabilities of graduates when presented with higher-level work compared to their European counterparts. The main difference comes down to those who have been taught with hands-on visual and tactile learning methods compared to those taught via traditional lecture and worksheet methods. [Snyder 1999[2]] As homeschoolers, we have the luxury of being able to work one-on-one with our learner. As a guide, we can be responsive to the specific needs and interests that motivate our learner as opposed to having to   public schooling where you would teach the same lesson in the same way to 35 students that are grouped together by age instead of by ability or interest.

In the next chapter, we will explore specific strategies for teaching math through visual learning, providing practical tips and techniques to help your child not just understand but enjoy math.

---

[2] Snyder, Rebecca Finley. "The Relationship between Learning Styles/Multiple Intelligences and Academic Achievement of High School Students." *The High School Journal*, vol. 83, no. 2, 1999, pp. 11–20. *JSTOR*, http://www.jstor.org/stable/40364506. Accessed 6 Aug. 2024.

CHAPTER FOUR

Homeschool Approaches - Finding the Right Fit

INTRODUCTION

Homeschooling offers a wealth of flexibility, allowing parents to tailor education to their learner's unique needs and learning styles. This flexibility is one of the key advantages of homeschooling, enabling parents to select or combine different approaches, such as project-based learning, unschooling, gameschooling, and others, to create a customized educational experience. However, it's important to remember that homeschooling is regulated at the state level, and the legal requirements for homeschooling vary widely across the United States. This chapter will explore different homeschooling methods and discuss how to meet legal requirements while documenting visual learning work to satisfy those requirements.

Understanding Legal Requirements by State

Each state has its own laws governing homeschooling, ranging from minimal oversight to more stringent requirements. Understanding your state's legal requirements is essential to ensure that your homeschooling program is compliant and that your learner's education is properly documented. You can find a link to your state's requirements through state based homeschooling groups or at the Home School Legal Defense Association (HSLDA) (https://hslda.org/legal)

* * *

46

- **Low-Regulation States:** Some states, like Texas, Oklahoma, and Indiana, have very few requirements for homeschooling families. In these states, there may be no need to notify the state or local authorities of your decision to homeschool, and there may be no mandated curriculum or assessments.

- **Moderate-Regulation States:** States like Colorado, Illinois, and New York require parents to submit a notice of intent to homeschool, keep records of attendance, and provide instruction in specific subjects. There may also be annual assessments or portfolio reviews.

- **High-Regulation States:** In states like Pennsylvania, New York, and Massachusetts, homeschooling families may need to submit detailed educational plans, keep comprehensive records, and have their learner's progress evaluated annually by a certified teacher or through standardized testing.

Key Steps to Compliance:

- **Research Your State's Laws:** Start by researching the homeschooling laws in your state. Websites like the Home School Legal Defense Association (HSLDA) provide up-to-date information on state requirements.

- **File Necessary Paperwork:** If your state requires it, be sure to file a notice of intent to homeschool with your local school district or state education department.

- **Understand Subject Requirements:** Make sure you are aware of any required subjects or instructional hours that must be covered in your homeschooling program.

Documenting Visual Learning to Meet Legal Requirements

When implementing visual learning strategies in your homeschool, it's important to document your learner's progress in a way that satisfies state requirements or to gather a portfolio of work for high level education applications. While visual learning can be highly effective, it may not always lend itself to traditional forms of documentation, such as written reports or standardized tests. Here are some strategies for documenting visual learning work:

1. **Portfolios:**
   - Visual Portfolios: Create a visual portfolio that showcases your learner's work. This can include photographs of projects, diagrams, drawings, mind maps, and screenshots of digital work. For example, if your learner uses Exploding Dots to solve math problems, include images of their work in the portfolio.
   - Annotated Visuals: Include annotations or brief descriptions with each visual piece to explain what the learner did, the concept they learned, and how it aligns with state requirements.
   - Progress Over Time: Document the progression of skills over time by including before-and-after examples of your learner's work. This can demonstrate how visual learning has helped them improve.

2. **Learning Journals:**
   - Daily or Weekly Logs: Keep a learning journal where you record daily or weekly activities, including details about the visual learning methods used. For instance, note that your learner used a graphic organizer to break down a complex science topic or created a mind map to plan a research project.
   - Reflections: Encourage your learner to add their own reflections in the journal. They can describe how they felt about a particular visual learning activity, what they learned, and what challenges they encountered.

3. **Photographic Evidence:**
   - Photo Documentation: Take photos of your learner engaging in hands-on visual activities, such as building a model, conducting an experiment, or drawing a diagram. Include these photos in your portfolio or learning journal as evidence of active learning.
   - Captioned Photos: Add captions to each photo to describe what is happening and how it relates to the learning objectives outlined in your state's

homeschooling requirements.

4. **Project-Based Documentation:**
   - Project Reports: Document larger visual learning projects with a project report. Include the project's objectives, the steps your learner took, and the final outcome. If your learner creates a visual model of a historical event, for example, document the research process, the materials used, and the final presentation.
   - Rubrics and Self-Assessments: Use rubrics to evaluate visual projects, and encourage your learner to complete self-assessments. This can provide additional documentation of their understanding and progress.

5. **Video and Audio Recordings:**
   - Video Presentations: Record your learner engaged with their work or explaining a concept they learned through visual methods. This can be especially useful for subjects like science or history, where your learner might explain the steps of an experiment or the significance of a historical event using visual aids.
   - Audio Descriptions: If your learner struggles with writing, consider recording audio descriptions of their visual work. They can verbally explain what they did, what they learned, and how the visual method helped them understand the material.
   - For non-verbal learners, a combination of video recordings showing work engagement, photos of your learner working through the concept steps and notebooking pages that provide annotations from your learner about what they learned that day can serve as effective documentation of work completed.

6. **Digital Portfolios:**
   - Online Portfolios: Consider creating a digital portfolio where you can store and organize visual learning work. This can be a convenient way to compile photos, videos, scanned drawings, and screenshots in one place. Platforms like Google Drive, Seesaw, or even a simple blog can serve as a digital portfolio.
   - Links to Resources: Include links to the online tools and apps your learner used for visual learning. For example, if your learner practiced math with an

interactive game, include a link to the game along with screenshots of their progress.

7. **Correspondence with Evaluators:**
   - Documentation for Annual Reviews: In states where an annual review or assessment by a certified teacher is required, compile all your visual documentation into a coherent package. Provide explanations of how visual learning techniques align with the state's educational goals.
   - Communication with Supervisors: If your state assigns a homeschooling supervisor or requires periodic check-ins, keep an open line of communication. Share how visual learning is being used and document their feedback on your methods.

Blending Homeschool Approaches and Satisfying Requirements

As you implement a blend of project-based learning, unschooling, gameschooling, and other visual learning strategies, it's important to remain mindful of state requirements. Even in less regulated states, maintaining detailed records can help ensure that your learner's education is comprehensive and that you are prepared if regulations change or if your circumstances require you to submit documentation.

By thoughtfully documenting your learner's progress and experiences with visual learning, you can satisfy legal requirements while also creating a rich, personalized educational journey that celebrates their unique learning style. This approach not only keeps you compliant but also provides a valuable record of your learner's growth and achievements, reflecting the true depth and breadth of their homeschooling experience. It's also helpful to have especially for older learners that may be interested in applying for college as you can utilize the records you keep to construct a transcript for their applications.

CASE STUDY: FINDING THE RIGHT FIT

* * *

Ethan's Journey through Different Homeschool Approaches

Ethan, a thirteen-year-old with Autism, faced significant challenges in traditional schooling. The rigid structure, the overwhelming sensory environment, and the emphasis on rote learning left him frustrated and disengaged. Recognizing that he needed a more flexible and personalized approach, Ethan's parents decided to homeschool him. They explored various educational methods, ultimately finding that a blend of gameschooling, unschooling, and experiential learning provided the best environment for Ethan to thrive.

Science: Experiential Learning with Project-Based Approaches
Ethan had always been fascinated by the natural world, but traditional science classes left him feeling disconnected from the subjects he loved. His parents decided to leverage his interest through experiential learning and project-based approaches.

For example, since Ethan expressed an interest in biology, he worked with his parents to choose ecology and ecosystems as a focus area for science. To study ecosystems, Ethan's parents designed a project to create a small terrarium. They began by visiting a local botanical garden, where Ethan observed different plants and ecosystems firsthand. They engaged with the staff and spoke with a volunteer Master Naturalist about the different conditions that different plants needed to thrive from the type of soil to the amount of shade. At home, he researched the components of a healthy ecosystem and selected the plants, soil, and other materials he needed for his terrarium.

As Ethan built and maintained his terrarium, he documented the growth of the plants, the behavior of any small insects he introduced, and the overall balance of the ecosystem. This hands-on project allowed Ethan to engage with scientific concepts like photosynthesis, food chains, and symbiosis in a way that was both meaningful and memorable. By observing the effects of his actions in real time, Ethan developed a deep understanding of the interdependence within ecosystems, far beyond what he could have learned from a textbook. Ethan used notebooking to create a documented journey of building an maintaining his ecosystem. He included photos of him with the Master Naturalist at the Botantical garden and photos of his terrarium from empty to thriving along with steps that he found worked to balance his ecosystem.

* * *

Math: Gameschooling for Engagement and Mastery

Math had always been a source of anxiety for Ethan. The abstract nature of numbers and operations, coupled with the pressure to perform under timed conditions, made him dread math lessons. To make math more accessible and enjoyable, Ethan's parents turned to gameschooling.

Ethan struggled with fractions, so his parents introduced him to a board game specifically designed to teach fraction concepts. The game involved dividing and combining pieces to form whole numbers, visually representing fraction addition and subtraction. As Ethan played, he began to see fractions not just as numbers on a page but as parts of a whole, which made the concepts click for him.

Additionally, they used digital math games that adapted to Ethan's skill level, providing him with instant feedback and rewards for his progress. These games turned what was once a stressful subject into a series of fun challenges that Ethan looked forward to. Over time, his confidence grew, and he began to see himself as capable of mastering math, even tackling more complex problems with enthusiasm. Once his confidence in his skill set grew, they could augment other learning methods to continue to expand his mathematical knowledge.

Astronomy: Unschooling and Self-Directed Exploration

Ethan had always been captivated by the stars. Traditional schooling provided little time for deep dives into topics of personal interest, so when his parents embraced unschooling as part of their homeschooling approach, they allowed Ethan to explore his passion for astronomy at his own pace.

Ethan's unschooling journey began with simple stargazing sessions in the backyard. His parents bought a beginner's telescope and some star charts, and Ethan spent evenings identifying constellations and planets. They downloaded apps that used his position to highlight what was in the night sky. This hands-on experience sparked his curiosity, leading him to watch documentaries about the solar system, black holes, and space exploration.

Instead of a rigid curriculum, Ethan's learning was guided by his

52

questions: How do stars form? What happens inside a black hole? Why does the moon change shape? His parents supported his interests by providing resources, such as astronomy books, apps for tracking celestial events, and even a visit to a planetarium. Ethan documented his questions and the results from his research and what he learned from his trips to the planetarium. He also created his own board game where players had to try and gather trading cards of the correct stars to construct a target constellation. Each card had facts and background on the stars or the fables and history behind each constellation name. The unschooling approach allowed Ethan to take ownership of his learning, diving deeply into topics that fascinated him without the constraints of traditional classroom expectations.

Blending Approaches for a Rich Learning Environment

By combining different homeschooling approaches—gameschooling for math, experiential learning for science, and unschooling for astronomy—Ethan's parents created a learning environment tailored to his unique strengths and interests. This blend allowed Ethan to engage with subjects in a way that was meaningful and enjoyable, fostering both his academic growth and his love for learning.

Daily Routine Example:

A typical day for Ethan might begin with a hands-on science experiment in the morning, followed by a math game session where he practices multiplication and division. After lunch, he might take a break to watch a space documentary, followed by an unscheduled period where he reads about the history of space exploration or sketches the phases of the moon.

This flexible, interest-driven approach enabled Ethan to explore subjects at his own pace, building knowledge in a way that made sense to him. The variety in methods also kept him engaged, as he could switch between different types of activities depending on his mood and energy levels.

Ethan's homeschooling journey is a testament to the power of personalized education. By embracing a mix of gameschooling, unschooling, and experiential learning, his parents created a rich, supportive environment that allowed Ethan to thrive. This approach not only helped him overcome the challenges he faced in traditional schooling but also empowered him to pursue his passions and develop a lifelong love for learning. Through this blend of approaches, Ethan discovered that learning could be both enjoyable and deeply fulfilling, laying the foundation for continued success in his educational journey.

PROJECT-BASED LEARNING

Project-based learning (PBL) is an instructional method where learners gain knowledge and skills by working on projects over extended periods. These projects are often complex, involving real-world problems and challenges that require critical thinking, collaboration, and creativity. PBL is particularly effective for visual learners because it naturally integrates visual and hands-on elements, making abstract concepts more concrete and understandable.

How It Works with Visual Learning:

- **Engagement through Visual Projects:** PBL naturally incorporates visual elements such as posters, models, presentations, and digital media. Learners can visualize their progress and outcomes, making learning more tangible and engaging.
- **Hands-On Activities:** Projects often involve building, creating, and experimenting, which are ideal for visual and kinesthetic learners. For example, a science project might include creating a visual model of the solar system.
- **Real-World Connections:** PBL connects learning to real-life scenarios, helping learners see the relevance of what they are learning. Visual aids and real-world applications enhance understanding and retention.

Example 1: History - Creating a Documentary on the American Revolution

Project Description:
Learners will create a short documentary about a key event in the American Revolution, such as the Boston Tea Party or the Battle of Yorktown. This project involves researching the historical context,

gathering visual and audio materials, and producing a video that tells the story from multiple perspectives.

- **Research and Visualization:** Learners start by researching their chosen event, using primary and secondary sources. They can create a storyboard that visually outlines the key moments of the event, helping them organize their ideas and plan their documentary.
- **Creating Visual Content:** Learners can use digital tools to create visual content, such as maps showing troop movements, re-enactments using digital avatars, or illustrations of historical figures. These visuals are incorporated into the documentary, making the historical narrative more engaging and easier to understand.
- **Presenting the Project:** The final documentary can be shared with peers, family, or a wider audience, allowing learners to showcase their understanding of the event through a visually rich medium. This project not only deepens their knowledge of history but also enhances their skills in research, digital media, and storytelling.

Example 2: Math - Designing a Small Business Budget

Project Description:

In this project, learners will design a budget for a hypothetical small business, such as a bakery, bookstore, or landscaping service. The project involves calculating costs, predicting revenue, and creating a financial plan that ensures profitability.

- **Visual Budget Planning:** Learners begin by listing all the potential expenses and income sources for their business. They can use visual aids like pie charts, bar graphs, and spreadsheets to represent these financial elements visually. For example, a pie chart could show the proportion of costs spent on ingredients, rent, and staff for a bakery.
- **Modeling Financial Scenarios:** Learners can create different financial scenarios (e.g., "What if sales increase by 10%?" or "How would an increase in rent affect the budget?") and use visual tools to model these changes. Graphs and charts can help them see how different variables impact the overall

financial health of the business.

- **Creating a Presentation**: The project culminates in a presentation where learners share their budget plan, using visual aids to explain their financial decisions. This approach not only helps them understand mathematical concepts like percentages, ratios, and profit margins but also connects math to real-world applications.

Example 3: Science - Investigating Environmental Impacts on Local Ecosystems

Project Description:

Learners will investigate the impact of human activity on a local ecosystem, such as a nearby river, forest, or wetland. The project involves conducting field research, collecting data, and presenting findings on how pollution, urbanization, or climate change is affecting the environment.

- **Field Research and Data Collection:** Learners start by visiting the chosen site to observe and collect data, such as water quality measurements, soil samples, or plant and animal populations. They can use cameras to document their observations, creating a visual record of the ecosystem.
- **Data Visualization:** Back in the classroom or at home, learners can create visual representations of their data, such as graphs showing pollution levels over time or maps indicating areas of deforestation. These visual tools help them analyze trends and draw conclusions about the environmental impact.
- **Creating a Visual Report:** The final product is a visual report that combines text, images, graphs, and maps to present their findings. This report can be shared with the community, raising awareness of local environmental issues and encouraging action.

Project-based learning (PBL) offers a versatile and engaging way to teach history, math, science, and other subjects, especially when combined with visual learning strategies. By incorporating real-world projects that require critical thinking, collaboration, and creativity, PBL not only makes learning more relevant and meaningful but also helps learners develop essential skills that will serve them well beyond the classroom. Whether it's creating a documentary, designing a budget, or investigating environmental impacts, PBL allows learners to explore subjects in depth, engage with the material visually, and connect their learning to the world around them.

UNSCHOOLING

Unschooling is a learner-centered approach that allows children to pursue their interests and learn at their own pace. This method emphasizes experiential, activity-based learning rather than a structured curriculum. As your learner's guide, your main focus is just providing as many resources and source material as you can for the topic. That may vary from art supplies to books. You can extend into learning opportunities at local museums or learning trips to visit a location for a particular historical event and take advantage of the local museums there dedicated to the time period or event of interest. For learners that struggle with executive function or become overwhelmed with too many options, you job as guide would be to provide a curated list of options that your learner can select from to continue exploring the targeted subject.

How It Works with Visual Learning:
- **Interest-Driven Learning:** Unschooling encourages exploration and discovery, which aligns well with visual learning. Children can delve into topics that fascinate them, using visual resources like documentaries, field trips, and interactive apps.
- Flexible and Adaptable: Without a rigid curriculum, unschooling can easily incorporate various visual learning tools and techniques. For instance, a child interested in marine biology might watch underwater documentaries and create visual journals of their findings.
- Natural Learning Environment: Unschooling often takes place in diverse environments, from home to nature, allowing for rich, visual experiences. Visual learners thrive in these dynamic settings where they can observe and interact with their surroundings.

* * *

Unschooling is highly adaptable to learners of different levels because it is inherently flexible and tailored to meet each learner where they are. Unlike traditional methods that adhere to a standardized curriculum, unschooling allows learners to pursue their interests and explore subjects at their own pace, making it accessible and engaging for learners of all abilities. Whether a learner is advanced in a particular area or needs more time to grasp certain concepts, unschooling provides the freedom to deepen their understanding or revisit topics as needed. For example, a learner with a strong interest in art might spend time mastering advanced techniques, while another who is just beginning to explore the subject can start with basic drawing exercises. Another learner may use stickers or digital tools to color or annotate. The adaptability of unschooling means that it can easily accommodate varying skill levels within the same subject, allowing each learner to progress in a way that feels natural and satisfying to them, fostering a love for learning that is both individualized and self-directed.

Example 1: Exploring History Through Visual Storytelling

Interest: History and Ancient Civilizations

Unschooling Approach:
A learner fascinated by ancient civilizations might begin by watching documentaries about Ancient Egypt, Greece, or Rome. This visual medium helps bring historical events and figures to life, making the past more relatable and engaging.

- **Visual Journals:** The learner can create a visual journal where they draw key artifacts, monuments, and symbols from these civilizations. They might sketch the Pyramids of Giza, the Parthenon, or Roman aqueducts, annotating each drawing with notes on its historical significance.
- **Recreating Artifacts:** For a more hands-on project, the learner could recreate historical artifacts using clay, papier-mâché, or other craft materials. For instance, they might sculpt a model of the Rosetta Stone or craft a replica of a Greek vase, learning about the culture and history behind each object as they work.
- **Field Trips:** If possible, visiting a local museum or historical site can provide an immersive experience. The learner can take

photographs, sketch what they see, and later create a visual presentation to share their findings with others.

- **Video Games:** There are lots of video games that have a learning component for different subjects or time periods. For example, ee have really enjoyed the Discovery Mode that some of the Assassin's Creed games have. In Origins, the discovery mode is completely story (and violence) free and allows the learner to walk through recreations of different ancient Egyptian cities and learn about construction techniques, trade, farming techniques, religion, technology used at the time, dress, education and transportation of goods and people between cities.

Example 2: Diving into Math with Real-World Applications

Interest: Architecture and Geometry

Unschooling Approach:

For a learner intrigued by architecture and design, math becomes a tool for exploring their interests. Without the constraints of a structured curriculum, they can dive into geometry by studying how shapes and angles are used in building structures.

- **Building Models**: The learner can start by building models of famous architectural structures using materials like Lego, cardboard, or 3D modeling software. As they construct, they can explore geometric concepts like symmetry, angles, and proportions.
- **Drawing Blueprints:** Encouraging the learner to draw blueprints for their own architectural designs helps them apply mathematical principles in a practical context. They can experiment with different shapes and layouts, learning how math influences the stability and aesthetics of buildings.
- **Exploring Geometry in Nature:** A walk through a park or urban area can become a lesson in geometry. The learner can photograph or sketch examples of geometric patterns in nature and architecture, such as the symmetry of leaves, the angles in bridges, or the curves of a spiral staircase. These observations can be compiled into a visual portfolio that highlights the intersection of math and the real world.

* * *

Example 3: Science Through Exploration and Observation

Interest: Ecology and Environmental Science

Unschooling Approach:
  A learner with a passion for nature and the environment can use unschooling to explore ecological concepts through direct observation and interaction with the natural world.

- **Creating a Nature Journal:** The learner can maintain a nature journal where they document their observations of local wildlife, plants, and ecosystems. Each entry might include sketches of animals, leaves, or insects, along with notes on behavior, habitat, and environmental conditions.
- **Environmental Fieldwork:** Regular visits to a local park, forest, or wetland allow the learner to engage in environmental fieldwork. They might track the changes in a particular area over time, documenting the impact of seasonal changes, human activity, or climate conditions. This hands-on approach helps them understand concepts like biodiversity, conservation, and the interdependence of ecosystems.
- **Citizen Science Projects:** The learner can participate in citizen science projects, where they contribute to larger scientific studies by collecting and submitting data on local species, weather patterns, or environmental changes. This involvement not only enhances their understanding of science but also connects them to a broader community of learners and researchers.

Unschooling offers a flexible and personalized approach to education that naturally integrates visual learning techniques. By allowing learners to explore their interests at their own pace, unschooling fosters deep engagement and a love of learning. Whether through visual storytelling in history, real-world math applications in architecture, or hands-on science exploration in nature, unschooling empowers learners to take charge of their education, creating meaningful connections between what they learn and the world around them. This approach not only caters to visual learners but also encourages creativity, curiosity, and critical thinking, laying the foundation for lifelong learning.

GAMESCHOOLING

Gameschooling uses games as the primary method of instruction, turning learning into an engaging and interactive experience. By incorporating both digital and physical educational games, gameschooling allows learners to explore various subjects in a way that feels like play, rather than traditional study. This method is particularly effective for visual learners, as it leverages graphics, animations, and visual problem-solving to make concepts come alive.

How It Works with Visual Learning:

- **Interactive and Engaging:** Games naturally engage visual learners through interactive graphics, animations, and visual problem-solving. Educational video games, board games, and card games can all be used to teach concepts in a fun and visually stimulating way.
- **Reinforcement of Concepts:** Games provide immediate feedback and repeated practice, helping to reinforce learning. Visual learners benefit from seeing their progress and understanding through game-based achievements and visuals.
- **Collaborative Learning:** Many educational games involve teamwork and competition, fostering social skills and collaborative problem-solving. Visual aids like game boards, pieces, and digital interfaces make learning collaborative and interactive.

Example 1: History - Learning Ancient Civilizations Through Board Games

Game: Timeline: Historical Events
To teach history, learners can use the board game Timeline: Historical Events, where they are challenged to place events from ancient civilizations in chronological order. The game includes visually rich cards depicting key historical moments, such as the construction

61

of the Pyramids or the founding of Rome.

- **Visual Connection**: As learners place each event in the timeline, they are exposed to the visual representation of these events, which helps them better remember the sequence of historical developments. The visual images on the cards reinforce the connection between the date and the event.
- **Storytelling:** Encourage learners to create a story around each event they place, imagining what life was like during that time. This helps deepen their understanding and engagement with history, turning facts into narratives.
- **Collaborative Play:** Learners can play in teams, discussing where each event belongs and reasoning together, which promotes collaborative learning and the sharing of historical knowledge.

Example 2: Math - Mastering Arithmetic with Digital Games

Game: DragonBox Algebra

To teach math, particularly arithmetic and early algebra, the digital game DragonBox Algebra transforms abstract concepts into visual puzzles that learners must solve to progress in the game. The game uses vibrant animations and interactive elements to make math concepts like balancing equations both fun and intuitive. As a personal note, my learner was able to understand the abstract concepts of combining algebraic like terms with DragonBox Algebra far before they even had their multiplication tables down. This purely visual approach is a fantastic way to integrate abstract concepts with very little complexity.

- **Visual Problem-Solving:** As learners manipulate shapes and symbols to solve algebraic puzzles, they develop a visual understanding of balancing equations. The game's design encourages them to see math not as numbers on a page, but as a dynamic, visual process.
- **Immediate Feedback:** The game provides instant feedback on each move, allowing learners to correct mistakes in real-time. This immediate reinforcement helps solidify their understanding and boosts their confidence in math.
- **Progress Tracking:** The game includes levels and

62

achievements that visually represent the learner's progress. These visual markers motivate learners to keep practicing and mastering more complex concepts.

Example 3: Science - Understanding Ecosystems Through Simulation Games

Game: Eco (A Simulation Game for Environmental Science)

In the simulation game Eco, learners must manage an ecosystem, making decisions that affect the environment, wildlife, and the community. This game introduces learners to ecological concepts through a visually immersive experience where every action has consequences.

- **Building and Managing Ecosystems:** Learners create and manage their own ecosystems, choosing which plants to grow, which animals to introduce, and how to balance human needs with environmental conservation. The game's visual interface allows learners to see the direct impact of their decisions on the ecosystem's health.
- **Cause and Effect**: As learners interact with the game, they observe how changes in one part of the ecosystem affect the whole. For example, overfishing might lead to a decline in fish populations, which in turn affects other species. These visual cause-and-effect relationships help learners grasp complex ecological systems.
- **Collaborative Science:** Learners can collaborate with others in a multiplayer setting, working together to create sustainable environments. This teamwork reinforces both social skills and scientific knowledge, with the game's visual feedback guiding their collective decision-making. [ref3]

Gameschooling offers a dynamic and interactive way to teach various subjects, especially when tailored to visual learners. By using educational games, both digital and physical, gameschooling transforms traditional learning into a visually engaging and hands-on

---

3 Ochs, Elinor, and Olga Solomon. "Autistic Sociality." *Ethos*, vol. 38, no. 1, 2010, pp. 69–92. *JSTOR*, http://www.jstor.org/stable/40603401. Accessed 6 Aug. 2024.

experience. Whether through the strategic placement of historical events in a timeline, the visual problem-solving in math, or the management of ecosystems in a simulation game, gameschooling makes learning fun, effective, and memorable. The immediate feedback and collaborative elements inherent in games further enhance the learning experience, allowing learners to explore, experiment, and succeed in a supportive and stimulating environment.

EXPERIENTIAL LEARNING

Experiential learning is an educational approach where learners gain knowledge and skills through direct experience, hands-on activities, and real-world engagement. This method emphasizes active participation and reflection, making learning deeply personal and meaningful. For visual learners, experiential learning is particularly effective because it involves seeing, doing, and interacting with the environment, which helps solidify abstract concepts into concrete understanding.

How It Works with Visual Learning:

- **Active Engagement:** Experiential learning engages learners directly with the material, allowing them to explore concepts through visual and physical means. Activities like field trips, experiments, and creative projects provide rich visual experiences that enhance understanding.
- **Real-World Applications:** By connecting learning to real-world situations, experiential learning helps learners see the relevance of what they are studying. Visual learners benefit from being able to observe and participate in activities that demonstrate the practical application of concepts.
- **Reflection and Analysis:** After engaging in an activity, learners reflect on their experiences, often through visual methods like journaling, drawing, or creating models. This reflection helps solidify learning and connects it to broader concepts.

Example 1: History - Immersive Historical Reenactment

* * *

To bring history to life, learners can participate in or observe a historical reenactment, such as a Civil War battle, a colonial market day, or a medieval festival. These events provide a visual and interactive experience that goes beyond textbook learning. Once on a trip to Boston, we participating in a reenactment of a meeting of Bostonians at Old South Meeting House. We even had speaking parts, upset about taxation on playing cards! Then we got to tour a replica of one of the ships and throw a bundle of tea overboard. We finished the experience by walking through a small historical gallery with portraits of historical figures and more information about the event and finished with a tasting of the specific teas that were thrown into Boston Harbor.

Activities:

- **Dressing the Part:** Learners can dress in period-appropriate costumes, immersing themselves in the historical context. This tactile and visual experience helps them connect with the era on a personal level.
- **Observing and Participating:** By observing or taking part in reenactments, learners can see historical events unfold, understand the daily lives of people from the past, and grasp the significance of key historical moments. They might engage in activities like cooking with historical recipes, practicing period-specific crafts, or participating in traditional games.
- **Reflective Journaling:** After the event, learners can create a visual journal where they document their experiences through sketches, photographs, and written reflections. They might draw scenes from the reenactment, annotate them with historical facts, and reflect on how the experience deepened their understanding of the time period.

One of my learners started a blog directed at time travelers to inform them about customs, dress, foods, and important historical events and the reasons behind people's actions so that the time travelers could blend in. This minute difference in objectives and audience really helped keep my learner engaged and observant. They delighted in understanding customs, clothing styles and behaviors that would have been understood as impolite in other times.

Example 2: Math - Learning Geometry Through Architecture Tours

* * *

Learners can explore the principles of geometry by visiting local architectural landmarks, such as cathedrals, bridges, or skyscrapers. This hands-on approach allows them to see how geometric concepts are applied in real-world structures.

Activities:
- **Guided Tours:** Learners can take guided tours of buildings that emphasize architectural features like symmetry, angles, and shapes. During the tour, they can sketch these features, noting how geometric principles contribute to the building's design and stability.
- **Interactive Models:** After the tour, learners can build their own models of the structures they observed using materials like clay, cardboard, or digital modeling software. This hands-on activity reinforces their understanding of geometric concepts like scale, proportion, and symmetry.
- **Reflective Analysis:** Learners can create a visual report that includes photographs, sketches, and models of the architectural landmarks they studied. They can analyze how geometry was used in each structure and reflect on how these principles are essential to architectural design.

We have used digital apps like Minecraft: Education edition to rebuild or to tour replicas of ancient and modern architecture as well as physical model building with paper crafts, Legos, or clay. One favorite collection my learner has started is of nano-lego scale models in the gift shops at places we visit in person. There are a surprising number of educational resources available online or if you ask for any resources that may exist at places that may host school trips. Even places like theme parks usually have educational handouts to learn about forces, motion, geometry, and materials strength for the park rides.

Example 3: Science - Investigating Local Ecosystems Through Field Studies

Learners can gain a deep understanding of environmental science by conducting field studies in local ecosystems, such as forests, wetlands, or urban green spaces. This immersive experience allows them to observe ecological interactions firsthand.

Activities:
- **Observation and Data Collection:** Learners can visit a local ecosystem to observe plant and animal life, weather patterns, and human impact. They might take photographs, record video, and collect samples (with appropriate permissions) to document their findings.
- **Hands-On Experiments:** In the field, learners can conduct experiments such as testing soil pH, measuring water quality, or tracking animal behavior. These hands-on activities help them understand scientific methods and principles in a real-world context.
- **Visual Reporting**: After completing their field studies, learners can create a visual report that includes maps, graphs, photos, and sketches to present their findings. This report can be shared with peers, teachers, or even local environmental organizations, making the learning experience both educational and impactful.

There are lots of opportunities to become a citizen scientist and contribute to ongoing monitoring of the health of your local ecosystems. For example, we use the free Seek app by iNaturalist when we are outside. It uses image recognition technology to identify the plants and animals that we spot on our walks. We can earn digital badges for seeing different types of birds, amphibians, plants, and fungi and participate in monthly observation challenges. This digital tool is a fun way for our learner to be more naturally curious and engaged in seeking. Out more information about the world around them.

Experiential learning provides a rich and dynamic approach to education that is particularly well-suited to visual learners. By engaging directly with the material through hands-on activities, field experiences, and real-world applications, learners can deepen their understanding and make meaningful connections between abstract concepts and tangible experiences. Whether through historical reenactments, architectural tours, or ecological field studies, experiential learning turns education into an active and engaging journey, fostering a deeper appreciation for the subjects being studied and helping learners develop critical thinking, problem-solving, and reflective skills. This approach not only enhances academic learning but also cultivates a lifelong love of exploration and discovery.

CLASSICAL EDUCATION

Classical education is a time-honored approach rooted in the trivium, a three-part process of training the mind that emphasizes rigorous academic discipline and the development of critical thinking skills. The trivium is divided into three stages: grammar, logic, and rhetoric. Each stage builds on the previous one, guiding learners from foundational knowledge to advanced reasoning and communication skills. While classical education is often associated with traditional methods, it can be adapted to support visual learners by incorporating visual memory aids, logical diagrams, and rhetorical presentations. Learners that tend to thrive with a lot of structure may find this to be a good approach. For learners that require more support or that struggle with communication, the classical learning approach is a difficult one for both learners and guides. However, if you participate in a local homeschool co-op or find a resource based in the classical approach, here are some ways of adapting it to include visual learning techniques.

How It Works with Visual Learning:

- **Visual Memory Aids**: The grammar stage involves memorization, where visual aids such as flashcards, charts, and diagrams can be highly effective.
- **Logical Diagrams:** The logic stage focuses on reasoning and critical thinking. Visual tools like Venn diagrams, flowcharts, and mind maps help learners organize and analyze information.
- **Rhetorical Presentations:** The rhetoric stage emphasizes communication skills. Visual learners can benefit from creating and delivering presentations using slideshows, visual aids, and multimedia.

Example 1: Grammar Stage - Building a Visual Timeline of Ancient

History

Stage Focus: Memorization and Foundational Knowledge

Classical Education Approach:
In the grammar stage, learners focus on acquiring foundational knowledge through memorization and repetition. For history, this might involve memorizing dates, events, and key figures from ancient civilizations.

Activities:
- **Creating a Visual Timeline:** To help learners memorize historical events, they can create a large visual timeline on a wall or poster board. This timeline can include images, dates, and brief descriptions of significant events from ancient history, such as the rise of the Egyptian Empire, the founding of Rome, and the construction of the Great Wall of China.
- **Flashcards with Visual Cues:** Learners can create flashcards that pair dates and events with images or symbols. For example, a flashcard for 44 B.C. might feature an image of Julius Caesar and a dagger to represent his assassination. These visual cues reinforce memorization by linking abstract information to memorable visuals.
- **Interactive Memory Games**: To make memorization more engaging, learners can use digital apps or interactive games that test their knowledge of historical events in a visually stimulating format. These tools can provide immediate feedback and help learners track their progress over time.

Example 2: Logic Stage - Analyzing Literature with Visual Tools

Stage Focus: Critical Thinking and Reasoning

Classical Education Approach:
During the logic stage, learners move beyond memorization to develop critical thinking and reasoning skills. In literature, this involves analyzing texts, identifying themes, and constructing logical arguments.

Activities:

- **Mind Mapping Themes**: Learners can use mind maps to visually organize the themes, characters, and plot points of a literary work. For example, while studying Shakespeare's Hamlet, they might create a mind map that links key themes like revenge, madness, and mortality to specific scenes and quotes from the play. This visual representation helps them see connections and develop deeper insights into the text.
- **Venn Diagrams for Comparative Analysis:** When comparing two works of literature or characters, learners can use Venn diagrams to visually represent similarities and differences. For example, they might compare and contrast the characters of Hamlet and Laertes, noting where their motivations overlap and where they diverge. This visual tool aids in organizing information logically and supports the development of comparative analysis skills.
- **Flowcharts for Plot Analysis**: Flowcharts can be used to trace the progression of a story's plot, showing how different events lead to specific outcomes. In studying The Odyssey, learners might create a flowchart that maps Odysseus's journey, highlighting the challenges he faces and the decisions he makes along the way. This helps them understand cause-and-effect relationships and the structure of narrative. You can also prepare cards for a plot progression and your learner can sequence the cards in the right order to demonstrate their learning.

Example 3: Rhetoric Stage - Crafting and Delivering Visual Presentations

Stage Focus: Communication and Expression

Classical Education Approach:
In the rhetoric stage, learners focus on refining their communication skills, particularly in constructing and presenting persuasive arguments. This stage builds on the knowledge and reasoning skills developed in the previous stages, emphasizing clarity, eloquence, and effective use of evidence.

Activities:
- **Designing a Visual Presentation**: Learners can use

presentation software like PowerPoint or Google Slides to create visual presentations on a topic of their choice. For instance, they might prepare a presentation on the causes and consequences of the French Revolution, using images, graphs, and bullet points to support their arguments. This allows visual learners to convey complex ideas through a combination of text and visuals, enhancing their ability to communicate effectively.

- **Multimedia Projects**: In addition to slideshows, learners can create multimedia projects that incorporate video clips, audio recordings, and infographics. For example, they might produce a short documentary on the philosophical ideas of the Enlightenment, combining interviews, historical footage, and animated diagrams to illustrate key concepts. This approach not only engages visual learners but also allows them to develop skills in media production and digital literacy.

- **Debates and Public Speaking with Visual Aids:** When participating in debates or delivering speeches, learners can use visual aids such as posters, charts, and handouts to reinforce their points and to organize their ideas. For example, in a debate on environmental policy, a learner might use a graph showing the rise in global temperatures to support their argument for stricter emissions regulations. The use of visuals in public speaking helps learners clarify their message and make a stronger impact on their audience. Using visuals to organize their research can also help with working memory to recall facts, figures and sources during a debate or speech.

Classical education, with its emphasis on the trivium, provides a structured and rigorous approach to learning that can be highly effective for visual learners when adapted appropriately. By incorporating visual memory aids in the grammar stage, logical diagrams in the logic stage, and rhetorical presentations in the rhetoric stage, classical education can cater to the strengths of visual learners while maintaining its focus on academic excellence and critical thinking. Through activities such as creating timelines, analyzing literature with mind maps, and delivering multimedia presentations, learners can engage deeply with the material, develop strong reasoning skills, and become confident communicators, fully embodying the principles of the classical education model.

* * *

MONTESSORI METHOD

The Montessori method emphasizes self-directed learning, hands-on activities, and collaborative play, encouraging learners to explore and discover at their own pace within a carefully prepared environment. This educational approach fosters independence, curiosity, and a deep love for learning. The Montessori environment is particularly well-suited for visual learners, as it is rich with visually engaging materials and activities that allow learners to interact with concepts in a tangible and meaningful way. I adapted many topics to Montessori methods for my low-verbal learner as it allowed him to demonstrate his learning without requiring verbal speech or writing.

How It Works with Visual Learning:
- **Prepared Environment:** Montessori classrooms are designed with visually appealing, hands-on learning materials that encourage exploration. Visual learners thrive in these environments where they can touch, see, and manipulate objects. For employing Montessori methods in a home-based environment, having a bookshelf with activity trays or bins for the learner to take out and an open space defined by a rug in the room for exploring those activities is a good adaptation.
- **Individualized Learning:** The Montessori approach tailors education to each learner's developmental stage and interests. Visual tools and activities are integral, allowing learners to learn visually and experientially.
- **Collaborative and Social Learning:** Montessori promotes collaborative learning through group activities and projects. Visual aids and shared resources enhance this collaborative environment.

Example 1: Math - Understanding Fractions with Manipulatives

Montessori Material: Fraction Circles
   In a Montessori classroom, math is taught through concrete materials that allow learners to visualize and physically manipulate abstract concepts. For fractions, Montessori uses fraction circles—

72

colored, segmented circles that represent different fractions (e.g., 1/2, 1/4, 1/8).

Activities:
- **Exploring Fractions Visually**: Learners begin by exploring the fraction circles, comparing the sizes of different segments. They can physically place one fraction over another to see how, for example, two 1/4 segments are equivalent to one 1/2 segment. This hands-on activity helps learners understand the relationships between different fractions in a visual and tactile way.
- **Building Fraction Equivalencies**: Learners can use the fraction circles to build equivalencies and practice addition or subtraction of fractions. For instance, they might combine 1/4 and 1/4 to form 1/2, visually seeing how fractions add up. This reinforces the concept through direct manipulation, which is especially helpful for visual learners.
- **Creating Fraction Charts:** As learners become more comfortable with fractions, they can create their own fraction charts, using colored paper or drawing software to visually represent the relationships between different fractions. This activity allows them to transition from concrete materials to more abstract representations, deepening their understanding.

Example 2: Language Arts - Learning Grammar with Montessori Grammar Symbols

Montessori Material: Grammar Symbols

Montessori uses a set of geometric shapes, each representing a different part of speech (e.g., a large black triangle for nouns, a small red circle for verbs). These symbols help learners visually categorize and understand the roles of words in sentences.

Activities:
- **Identifying Parts of Speech:** Learners can start by reading simple sentences and placing the corresponding grammar symbols above each word. For example, in the sentence "The cat runs fast," they would place a black triangle above "cat," a red circle above "runs," and a small orange triangle above "fast." This visual activity helps learners grasp the function of

each word in a sentence.

- **Building Complex Sentences:** As learners progress, they can use the grammar symbols to construct more complex sentences, visually organizing their thoughts. This activity encourages them to experiment with sentence structure, enhancing their understanding of grammar.
- **Creating Grammar Books:** Learners can compile a "grammar book," where they write sentences and diagram them using the Montessori grammar symbols. This personalized resource allows them to review and reinforce their understanding of grammar in a visually engaging way. You can also incorporate sentences that focus on their interest areas to increase their engagement.

Example 3: Science - Exploring Botany Through Leaf and Flower Puzzles

Montessori Material: Botany Puzzles

In Montessori education, science is introduced through exploration of the natural world, using hands-on materials that allow learners to see and touch what they are studying. Botany puzzles, which feature dissected parts of leaves, flowers, and trees, are a key tool for teaching about plant biology.

Activities:
- **Assembling Plant Parts:** Learners can start by assembling the puzzles, which include the different parts of a leaf or flower (e.g., petiole, blade, stamen, petal). As they fit the pieces together, they learn the names and functions of each part, reinforcing their understanding through visual and tactile interaction.
- **Creating Botanical Drawings:** After working with the puzzles, learners can draw their own diagrams of the plants they've studied, labeling each part. This activity encourages them to apply what they've learned and helps reinforce their knowledge through artistic expression.
- **Field Studies and Nature Journals:** Learners can take their knowledge outdoors, identifying and collecting real leaves and flowers. They can press these specimens into a nature journal and draw or photograph them, adding notes about each

plant's characteristics. This activity connects classroom learning to the natural world, making science tangible and relevant.

The Montessori method, with its emphasis on self-directed, hands-on learning, provides an ideal environment for visual learners. Through carefully designed materials and activities, learners are encouraged to explore and understand concepts in a way that aligns with their natural learning style. Whether they are manipulating fraction circles, using grammar symbols, or assembling botany puzzles, Montessori learners engage deeply with the material, developing a strong foundation in math, language, and science. The method's focus on individualized learning and collaborative play further enriches the experience, allowing each learner to thrive in an environment that respects their pace and interests. By adapting the Montessori approach to visual learning, educators can create a nurturing and effective educational journey that fosters both academic excellence and a lifelong love of learning.

WALDORF EDUCATION

Waldorf education focuses on holistic development, integrating academics, arts, and practical skills. This approach emphasizes creativity, imagination, and experiential learning, aiming to nurture the intellectual, emotional, and physical aspects of each learner. Waldorf education is particularly well-suited for visual learners, as it incorporates artistic expression, storytelling, and hands-on activities that make learning tangible and meaningful.

How It Works with Visual Learning:

- **Artistic Expression:** Waldorf education incorporates art, music, and drama into the curriculum. Visual learners benefit from drawing, painting, and performing, which make abstract concepts more concrete.
- **Storytelling and Visualization:** Lessons often begin with storytelling, which engages learners' imaginations and visual thinking. Visual aids such as illustrations and puppetry

enhance storytelling.

- **Hands-On Activities:** Waldorf emphasizes practical skills and hands-on activities, which align well with visual learning. Activities like gardening, crafting, and building help learners learn through doing.

Example 1: History - Bringing Ancient Cultures to Life Through Art

In Waldorf education, history is taught through a combination of storytelling, art, and hands-on projects that bring ancient cultures to life. Learners explore historical periods by engaging their imaginations and creating visual representations of the past.

Activities:
- **Drawing and Painting Historical Scenes:** After listening to a story about ancient Egypt or Greece, learners can draw or paint scenes from the period, such as the construction of the pyramids or a Greek marketplace. This artistic activity allows them to visualize and internalize the historical content in a personal and meaningful way.
- **Creating Historical Artifacts:** Learners can create replicas of historical artifacts, such as clay tablets with cuneiform writing, Egyptian jewelry, or Greek pottery. These hands-on projects help learners connect with history on a tactile level, making the past more relatable and engaging.
- **Mural Projects:** Learners can work together with their guides and family members participating to create large murals depicting a historical timeline or a significant event from history. This collaborative family project not only reinforces historical knowledge but also fosters teamwork and a sense of learner accomplishment and inclusion as a part of a team.

Example 2: Science - Exploring the Natural World Through Observation and Artistic Representation

In science, Waldorf education emphasizes the study of nature through direct observation, artistic representation, and experiential learning. Learners are encouraged to develop a deep connection with the natural world by engaging all their senses.

* * *

Activities:
- **Nature Drawing Journals:** Learners can maintain a nature journal where they regularly sketch plants, animals, and landscapes they observe during outdoor excursions. This practice hones their observation skills and helps them develop a keen eye for detail, while also allowing them to express their experiences artistically.
- **Painting the Seasons:** As learners study the changing seasons, they can create paintings that capture the colors, moods, and characteristics of each season. This artistic activity not only enhances their understanding of natural cycles but also fosters an appreciation for the beauty of the natural world.
- **Botanical Studies with Watercolors:** While studying botany, learners can use watercolors to paint detailed illustrations of plants and flowers. This artistic process helps them focus on the form, structure, and function of different plant species, reinforcing their scientific knowledge through visual and creative expression.

Example 3: Math - Understanding Geometry Through Form Drawing and Hands-On Activities

Waldorf education introduces mathematical concepts, particularly geometry, through form drawing and hands-on activities that emphasize the beauty and patterns found in mathematical forms. This approach encourages learners to see math not just as numbers but as a creative and visual discipline.

Activities:
- **Form Drawing:** Learners can engage in form drawing, where they create intricate geometric patterns and shapes with freehand. This practice develops their fine motor skills and spatial awareness, while also helping them internalize geometric principles through repetitive and artistic expression.
- **Geometric Art Projects:** As learners progress in their study of geometry, they can create art projects that explore the properties of different shapes. For example, they might design mandalas or tessellations, using rulers and compasses to create precise and symmetrical patterns. This activity bridges the gap between artistic creativity and mathematical logic.

- **Building Geometric Models**: Learners can construct geometric models using materials like wood, clay, or paper. For example, they might build a series of polyhedra or explore the relationships between different types of triangles. These hands-on projects allow learners to physically manipulate and explore geometric concepts, deepening their understanding through tactile and visual experiences.

Waldorf education, with its emphasis on holistic development and integration of the arts, offers a rich and supportive environment for visual learners. By incorporating artistic expression, storytelling, and hands-on activities into the curriculum, Waldorf education makes abstract concepts more concrete and accessible. Whether learners are drawing historical scenes, painting botanical studies, or engaging in form drawing, they are encouraged to explore the world visually and creatively. This approach not only nurtures their intellectual growth but also fosters a deep appreciation for beauty, nature, and the interconnectedness of all knowledge. By adapting Waldorf methods to support visual learning, educators can create an enriching educational experience that honors the unique ways in which each learner sees and understands the world.

PRACTICAL TIPS FOR IMPLEMENTING DIFFERENT APPROACHES

Practical Tips for Implementing Different Approaches

1. **Assess Your Child's Needs and Interests:** Choose a homeschooling approach or blend elements from different approaches that aligns with your child's learning style, strengths, and interests. Flexibility and adaptability are key.
2. **Combine Approaches:** Don't be afraid to mix and match different methods to find what works best for your child. For example, you can combine project-based learning with gameschooling for a more comprehensive approach on a history topic and switch to hands-on model building for a science topic.
3. **Use Visual Tools and Resources:** Regardless of the approach,

incorporate visual tools and resources to enhance learning. Interactive apps, visual aids, and hands-on activities can be integrated into any method.

4. **Create a Supportive Environment:** Ensure that your homeschooling environment supports the chosen approach. This might include setting up a dedicated learning space, providing access to necessary materials, and fostering a positive, encouraging atmosphere.

CONCLUSION

There are numerous homeschooling approaches, each with distinct strengths and strategies. By exploring and understanding these different methods, you can discover the best fit for your learner's unique needs and learning style. Visual learning strategies can be seamlessly integrated into any approach, enhancing both comprehension and engagement, particularly for neurodivergent learners.

In the next section, we will delve into how to specifically adapt lessons for mathematics, science, and the humanities, offering practical tips and techniques for guiding your neurodiverse learner. Instead of breaking down topics by grade levels, I will blend various homeschooling approaches, from unschooling to classical education methods, allowing for a more tailored learning experience. Since each learner progresses at their own unique pace, you may find that your learner excels in advanced mathematics while facing challenges in reading due to working memory issues. Traditional public schools often group students by age and assign grade levels accordingly, but this correlation doesn't always align with a learner's readiness. Focusing strictly on grade-level objectives can either limit your learner or fail to provide the necessary material for skill progression. To address your learner's specific educational needs, I will present techniques that are adaptable to all learners and strategies for applying visual learning methods to various educational topics.

PART TWO

SUBJECT SPECIFIC STRATEGIES

CHAPTER FIVE

Visual Mathematics: Visual Math: From Numbers to Confidence

INTRODUCTION

Math can be a challenging subject for many children, but for neurodivergent learners, traditional methods often fall short. Visual math strategies can transform this experience, making math more accessible, understandable, and enjoyable. This chapter will explore general techniques for visual math, the neuroscience behind why these techniques work, and how visual learning strengthens mathematical understanding. Instead of approaching mathematics from a grade-level view, this will explore the topic from a concept-level view. As our leaners don't always follow the public-school progression of topics, it's best to meet your learner where they are. Whether they have an affinity for numbers or if they struggle with them, all learners benefit from focused math instruction at their level.

PERSONAL STORIES: VISUAL MATH SUCCESS

Emma's Journey with Visual Math

Emma, a middle schooler with dyslexia and ADHD, struggled with reading comprehension and math in a traditional classroom. For a variety of reasons, her parents decided to homeschool her and after trying some packaged all-in-one homeschool programs, they finally found a good match for Emma focusing on visual learning techniques. They used graphic novels to make reading enjoyable and employed mind maps to help Emma organize and recall information.

For math, Emma's parents introduced visual aids like colorful charts and interactive math apps. These tools helped her understand and solve problems, transforming her math experience from frustration to confidence. By relying on visual techniques and employing interactive visual tools, Emma could complete her concept goals with less frustration and her confidence soared. Emma's ability to visualize mathematical concepts improved significantly, and her interest in math grew.

One of the significant challenges Emma faced in her math studies was understanding and performing long division. The traditional method, which relies heavily on procedural steps and abstract reasoning, was particularly difficult for Emma due to her dyslexia. She struggled to keep the steps in order and often became frustrated when she couldn't see how the numbers were interacting with each other. This led to a cycle of frustration and avoidance, where Emma would become anxious whenever a division problem appeared.

To help Emma overcome this challenge, her parents introduced a visual learning technique called "Exploding Dots." Exploding Dots is a mathematical tool that transforms abstract concepts like division into visual and interactive experiences. The tool uses a simple, engaging visual representation where dots "explode" to form new groups, making it easier to understand how division works.

Emma was given a problem that required her to divide a three-digit number by a single-digit number, something she had struggled with multiple times before. In a traditional setting, she would have to remember the steps of long division, place the numbers correctly, and perform operations without losing track. The abstract nature of the process made it difficult for her to grasp the underlying concepts.

With Exploding Dots, the problem was represented visually. Instead of just writing out numbers, Emma could see the dots in different "boxes" or "places," representing units, tens, and hundreds. As she worked through the problem, she could see the groups of dots "explode" and transfer to the next place value, giving her a concrete understanding of what division actually means. This visual and interactive process allowed her to see the relationship between the numbers and made the division process clear and intuitive. For example, in the division example shown below works out $248 \div 11 = 22$ (2 groups of 11 tens and 2 groups of 11 ones) with 6 (ones) left over, or $248 = 22 \times 11 + 6$. Emma could work out long division problems all visually and usually in less time than it was requiring even her parents to work out by hand using the traditional arithmetic techniques they learned. By turning the problems into a game, Emma "won" more rounds as the problems got more complex. There was less memorization required of times tables and she was so delighted in beating her parents with her newfound speed, she requested more complex problems to do for fun!

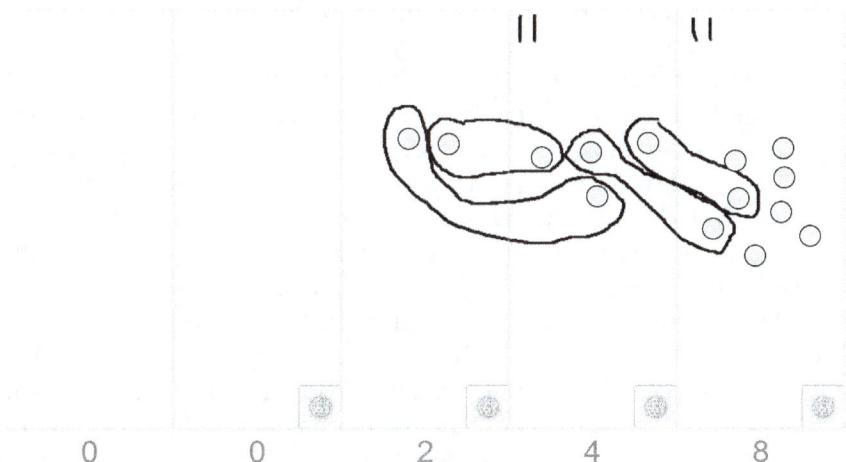

Example Division of 248 by 11 with Exploding Dots as implemented on GuzintaMath.com

By visualizing division using Exploding Dots, Emma was able to complete her division problems without the usual frustration. She could see exactly where each part of the number was going and why. This visual representation not only made division easier for her but also helped her understand the concept at a deeper level. Over time, as she practiced with this method, her confidence in tackling division problems grew, and she no longer felt anxious when faced with similar challenges. Emma's success with visual learning methods marked a turning point in her math education, showing her that with the right tools and techniques, she could master even the most difficult concepts.

GENERAL TECHNIQUES FOR VISUAL MATH

Visual learners benefit from seeing concepts in action. Here are some key techniques to explore for teaching math visually at any level:

Manipulatives

Physical objects like blocks, beads, and counters can help children visualize mathematical concepts. Anything you can find to represent numbers can make addition and subtraction more tangible. The world is your oyster here. Find a manipulative that your learner finds sensory joy in. Does the clink of metal make them happy? Use washers or pennies. Marbles can make a satisfying sound when they are grouped together. Blocks of all kinds can help make place value and early additional and subtraction concepts more concrete. As your math journey grows, you can adapt your manipulatives to vary by size or color to start indicating place value. Physical fraction bars or pies math skill wrap-up keys can enable a child to demonstrate their knowledge without paying the mental processing load or requiring the small motor skills needed for writing down answers to spatial problems with numerals.

* * *

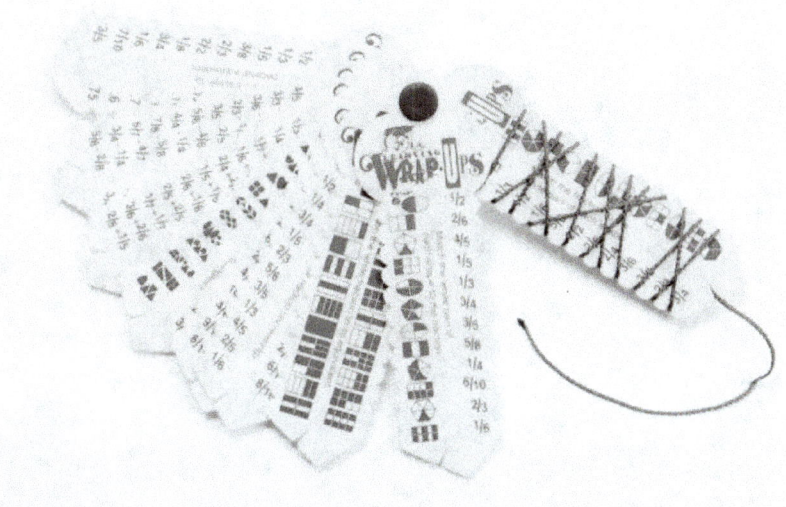

Fraction Wrap-Up Keys

Math is better learned, retained and understood through visual methods as it is primarily dealing with either concrete things or abstract concepts. If you think about your early human history classes, you might remember that early mathematics started with tallying objects and then marking hashtags or tally marks on objects like bones, walls, and clay tablets. The concept of counting doesn't have to take the form of arabic numerals like 1, 2, 3, etc. For early learners we can represent these concepts quite visually of course with nearly anything from blocks to pennies to marbles. For more abstract math or math that requires more "stuff", using a marble to represent "1" would require quite a basketful of marbles to try and describe 52*31. Of course that doesn't mean that there are not other visual techniques to describe higher-order mathematics or larger numbers. Many of our neurodiverse learners process information in a visual way, thinking more in pictures than in words. An abacus is a wonderful tool that helps many learners bridge communication gaps by being able to show that they understand a concept and can be used for higher order arithmetic. They also visualize arithmetic concepts like place value quite easily and simply. Finding the best fit for your learner will help to open up the world of mathematics to them.

* * *

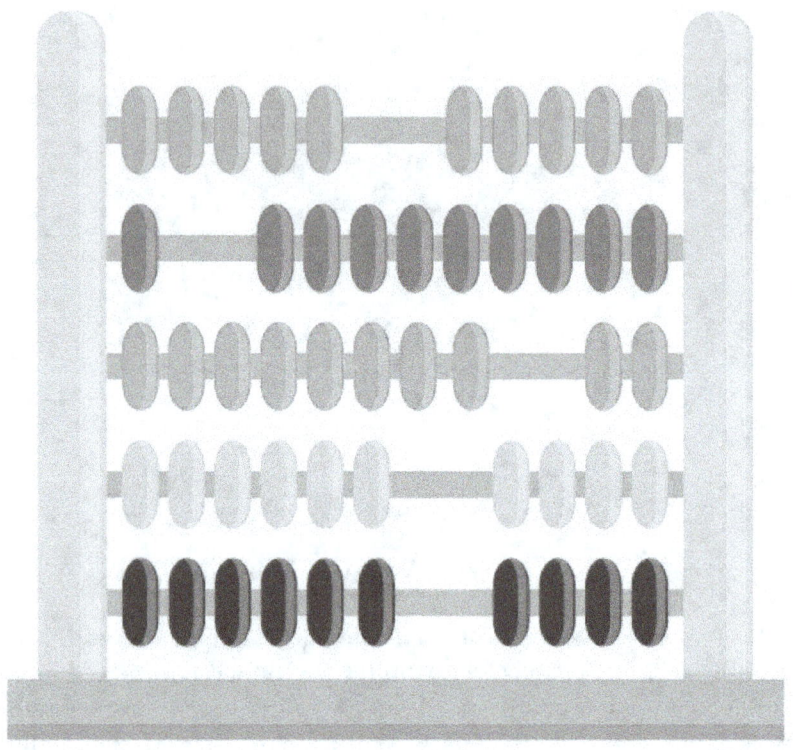

An abacus showing 44,295

Visual Aids

Charts, diagrams, and color-coded materials can illustrate abstract concepts. Graphs can make data analysis more comprehensible, and drawing colored fraction bars can clarify fractions and decimals. Visual aids are powerful tools that can enhance a learner's understanding by providing a visual representation of concepts. These tools can help make abstract ideas more concrete, enabling learners to grasp complex topics more easily. Visual aids can take many forms, from charts and diagrams to flashcards and graphic organizers. The key is to find visual aids that resonate with your learner and align with their sensory preferences.

For example, colorful charts and graphs can help learners track their progress or understand trends in data. Flashcards with bold images and clear text can reinforce vocabulary or mathematical concepts.

Graphic organizers, such as mind maps or flow charts, can break down information into manageable chunks, making it easier for learners to compare concepts, process new ideas, and retain information.

If your learner enjoys tactile experiences, consider using textured visual aids, such as raised-line graphs or 3D models, which combine visual and sensory input. Remember, the goal is to use visual aids that not only clarify concepts but also engage your learner's senses, making learning both effective and enjoyable.

Interactive Learning

Interactive learning is a dynamic approach that actively engages learners in the educational process, making learning more engaging, hands-on, and effective. Instead of passively receiving information, learners interact directly with the material, which can significantly enhance their understanding and retention of concepts. This approach is especially beneficial for neurodivergent learners who may need more engaging and sensory-rich experiences to fully grasp new ideas.

Online tools, apps, and educational games are excellent resources for interactive learning. These platforms often provide immediate feedback, allowing learners to correct mistakes and build confidence as they go. For example, math apps that let learners solve problems by dragging and dropping numbers, or online games that require solving puzzles to advance levels, can turn learning into a fun and rewarding experience. Check out the math apps and websites in the appendix for my recommendations on tools that really condense the concepts into concrete visual ways.

Beyond digital tools, interactive learning can also include hands-on activities such as using whiteboards to solve problems in real-time, participating in virtual labs for science experiments, or engaging in collaborative group projects where learners can brainstorm, debate, and build ideas together. These activities not only make learning more engaging but also help develop critical thinking, problem-solving, and teamwork skills. Think about setting up a pretend cafe with a menu of your learner's favorite snacks. They can help you come up with a menu, prices, and you can decorate a small table. While working on all of these practical life skills, they are learning math without it feeling like a chore. By taking your order and working with payments for items, you can increase or decrease the complexity of your home cafe to meet your learner where they are. Payments could be in the form of whole numbered counters or you can work on decimals or place value problems just with variations to menu pricing.

Incorporating physical movement can also enhance interactive learning. Activities like scavenger hunts for math problems hidden around the house or building models to represent scientific concepts can help learners connect physically with the material, making it more memorable. When my learner was non-verbal, I would use the small fitness trampoline in our sensory area to create a multiple choice game. I would ask a question and then put two or three answers on the wall via sticky notes or on the trampoline with paper options. I'd ask a question like which one shows how many are left if you had 5 nuggets and ate 2. This physicality takes advantage of the benefits that this heavy joint work brings to regulating the nervous system and focusing the mind and it doesn't require a learner to be verbal or even be able to read. This trampoline technique can be used for any age learner and you can increase the complexity of the problems to match your learner's objectives. By making learning a more active process, you cater to a wide range of learning styles and create a more inclusive educational environment that encourages exploration and curiosity.

Drawing and Sketching

Drawing and sketching are powerful tools for helping learners visually process and understand mathematical concepts. By encouraging learners to draw problems and solutions, you tap into their creative and visual strengths, making abstract concepts more concrete and easier to grasp. This method can be particularly effective for neurodivergent learners who may struggle with traditional, text-based methods of learning math.

When learners encounter word problems, they can often feel overwhelmed by the amount of text and the need to translate words into mathematical operations. By sketching out the scenario described in the word problem, learners can break down the information into manageable pieces. For example, if a word problem involves distributing apples among friends, the learner can draw the friends and the apples, visually organizing the data before applying any mathematical operations. This process helps them better understand the relationships and quantities involved, making it easier to decide on the appropriate mathematical approach.

Equations can often seem abstract, especially when they involve variables and complex operations. By sketching visual representations of equations, learners can see the balance and structure more clearly. For instance, when solving an equation like $3x + 5 = 20$, learners can draw a balance scale with the equation represented on each side. On one side, they might draw three question boxes representing $3x$ and a stack of five units representing $+5$. On the other side, they could draw a stack of twenty units. This visual approach allows them to physically see the need to balance the equation by subtracting the same amount from both sides and then dividing the rest equally to figure out what fits in each box (or what the value of "x" is).

* * *

Geometry naturally lends itself to drawing and sketching. When learners draw shapes, angles, or graphs, they engage in a form of visual reasoning that helps them understand the properties and relationships of geometric figures. Sketching triangles, for example, allows learners to explore concepts like the Pythagorean theorem by visually identifying the relationships between the sides of the triangle. Similarly, drawing graphs of linear equations helps learners see the relationship between the algebraic equation and its geometric representation.

Drawing and sketching can also be used to encourage creative problem-solving. When faced with a complex problem, learners can sketch out different possible solutions, exploring various approaches visually before committing to a particular method. This process not only enhances their understanding but also builds confidence in their ability to tackle challenging problems.

Drawing and sketching can be combined with other visual tools like graphic organizers or mind maps to further enhance learning. For example, a learner might sketch a visual representation of a math problem and then use a mind map to connect it to related concepts or steps needed to solve it. This integration of visual techniques reinforces understanding and helps learners see the bigger picture.

By incorporating drawing and sketching into math lessons, you create an interactive and engaging learning experience that caters to the strengths of visual learners. This approach not only makes math more accessible but also fosters a deeper, more intuitive understanding of mathematical concepts, helping learners develop strong problem-solving skills and confidence in their abilities.

Mind Maps

Mind maps are a powerful visual tool that can help learners break down complex problems into simpler, more manageable parts. By using mind maps, learners can organize information, identify relationships between different elements, and gain a clearer understanding of the problem at hand. This technique is particularly effective for neurodivergent learners who benefit from visualizing concepts and seeing how they connect to one another. This is a technique that can be utilized for any concept in any subject and you can fill in the elements with text, pictures, or drawings.

CONCEPT MAP

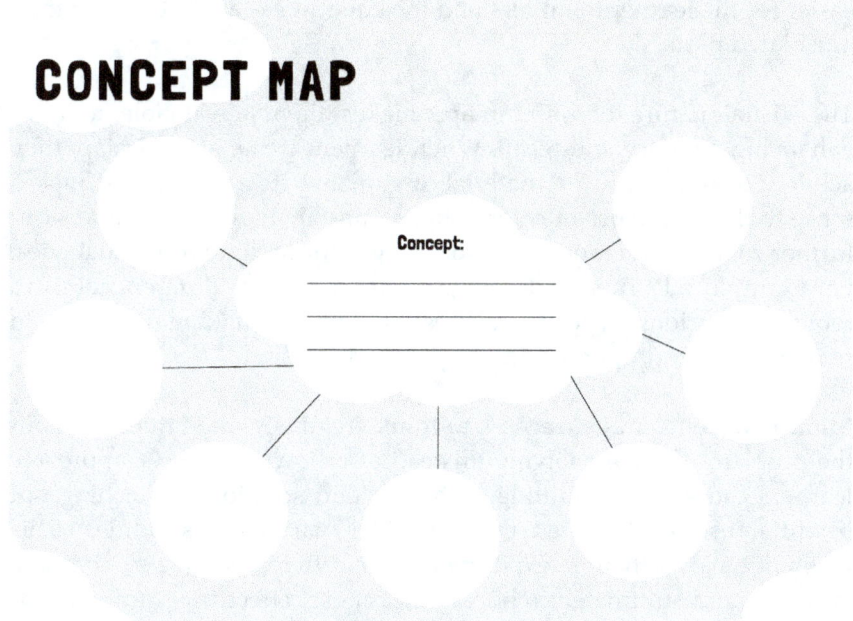

Mind Map Template

When faced with a complicated math problem or a multi-step process, learners can easily become overwhelmed by the sheer amount of information they need to process. A mind map allows them to start with the central concept or problem and then branch out into smaller, more digestible parts. For instance, if a learner is working on a word problem involving multiple operations (addition, subtraction, multiplication), they can place the main problem in the center of the mind map and then create branches for each step required to solve it. This visual breakdown helps them focus on one piece of the puzzle at a time, reducing cognitive load and making the problem more approachable.

Mind maps are excellent for showing the relationships between different elements of a problem. For example, in algebra, a learner might create a mind map to explore how different variables interact in an equation. By placing the equation in the center and drawing branches to represent each variable, the learner can visually track how changes in one variable affect the others. This visual representation reinforces the concept of interdependence between elements, making it easier for the learner to understand the equation as a whole rather than as isolated parts.

The visual nature of mind maps makes them a valuable tool for enhancing memory and recall. When learners create a mind map, they actively engage with the material, organizing it in a way that makes sense to them. The use of colors, shapes, and images in mind maps can further reinforce memory by associating information with visual cues. For example, a learner studying geometry might use different colors to represent various types of angles or shapes, making it easier to remember their properties during problem-solving.

Mind maps encourage learners to think creatively and critically about the problems they are solving. Instead of following a linear approach, learners can explore multiple pathways and solutions, branching out in different directions as they consider various possibilities. This flexibility allows them to experiment with different strategies, compare options, and ultimately choose the most effective solution. For instance, in a problem involving resource allocation, a learner might use a mind map to brainstorm all possible resources, assess their availability, and then connect them to the different needs they must meet.

Mind maps can be integrated with other visual tools, such as graphic organizers or flow charts, to provide a comprehensive approach to problem-solving. For example, a learner might start with a mind map to break down a complex problem and then use a flow chart to detail the steps needed to solve it. This combination of visual strategies reinforces understanding and helps learners navigate the problem-solving process more effectively.

Mind maps can also be used in collaborative learning settings, where learners work together or are working together with their guide to solve a problem. By collectively building a mind map, learners can share their ideas, see how their thoughts connect, and build on each other's contributions. This collaborative approach not only enhances learning but also fosters teamwork and communication skills.

* * *

By incorporating mind maps into math lessons, you provide learners with a versatile and powerful tool for organizing their thoughts, visualizing relationships, and breaking down complex problems. This approach not only makes challenging concepts more accessible but also encourages deeper understanding, critical thinking, and creativity, helping learners develop strong problem-solving skills and confidence in their abilities.

THE NEOUROSCIENCE BEHIND VISUAL LEARNING

Understanding the neuroscience behind visual learning can help explain why these techniques are so effective for neurodivergent learners.

- **Visual Processing in the Brain**: The brain processes visual information more efficiently than text or auditory information. The occipital lobe, responsible for visual processing, can handle large amounts of data quickly, making visual learning a powerful tool.
- **Dual Coding Theory:** This theory suggests that combining visual and verbal information enhances learning and memory. When children see and hear information simultaneously, they create stronger connections and retain information better.
- **Working Memory and Cognitive Load**: Visual aids can reduce cognitive load by breaking down complex information into manageable chunks. This is especially beneficial for children with working memory challenges, as it allows them to process information more effectively.

Visual learning not only makes math more accessible but also strengthens overall understanding in several ways:

- **Concrete Representation of Abstract Concepts**: Visual tools provide a tangible way to understand abstract mathematical concepts. For example, using visual fraction bars helps children see and compare fractions, making the concept less abstract.

- **Enhanced Problem-Solving Skills**: Visual learning encourages active engagement and exploration. By visualizing problems, children can approach them from different angles and develop stronger problem-solving skills.
- **Improved Retention and Recall**: Visual representations aid in memory retention. Children are more likely to remember information presented visually, which enhances their ability to recall and apply mathematical concepts in different contexts.
- **Increased Engagement and Motivation**: Visual learning can make math more interesting and enjoyable. Interactive tools and colorful visual aids capture children's attention and keep them motivated to learn.

IMPLEMENTING VISUAL MATHEMATICS

Polynomial Factoring Example Lesson Plan Using Visual Math Techniques

Let's explore how you can implement visual math techniques, such as Exploding Dots, to help your learner grasp the concept of a more advanced concept like polynomial factoring to show that visual math techniques using the same counters you can use with early learners can carry your learner through high school and even college level mathematics.This lesson can be expanded, simplified, or adapted depending on your learner's level and interest. Exploding Dots starts with helping learners visually understand place value in elementary level math including subtraction, addition, division and multiplication. However, we are going to jump up into high school level algebra to show that visual math techniques can transform even complex algebraic processes into engaging and comprehensible learning experiences, helping your learner move from confusion to confidence. If you find this example difficult to follow at first, seek out an intro video[4] on the technique. Once the idea clicks for you, it may open up a

---

[4] https://youtu.be/bvglHQk-Ygs?si=SMPG_Rh-twn9DvhW

96

whole new way of approaching advanced mathematics for the visual leaner.

Polynomial Factoring Example Lesson Plan:

1. Introduction to the Concept:
- Start by introducing the idea of polynomial factoring in a way that connects with your learner's existing knowledge. For an early introduction, you might compare polynomial factoring to breaking down numbers into their prime factors. Explain that just as numbers can be factored into smaller parts (e.g., 12 into 2, 2, and 3), polynomials can also be broken down into simpler expressions.
- Use simple visuals on a whiteboard or paper or counters like pennies or washers, showing how a number like 12 can be split into its prime number factors. For any non-prime number, you can arrange your counters into a block. Each dimension of your block equals a multiple to build 12 like 4 columns and 3 rows which translates to 4x3. You can extend this if you are able to evenly divide any of the columns or numbers of rows into additional equal groups, then you are breaking those factors down to even smaller pieces. Below, I show 12 breaking down into 2x2x3. Next, explain you will extend this same idea to polynomials.

* * *

12 counters = 2 x 2 x 3

2. Using Exploding Dots to Visualize Factoring:
- Introduce the Exploding Dots technique as a way to visually represent the factoring process. If your learner is new to Exploding Dots, start with a brief review of how it works. Show them how numbers or algebraic expressions can be broken down into dots, and how these dots can be "exploded" or combined to form simpler groups.
- Present a simple polynomial, such as $x^2 + 5x + 6$, and demonstrate how this expression can be represented with dots in different "boxes" (e.g., x^2 in the first box, $5x$ in the second, and 6 in the third).

$$x^2 + 5x + 6$$

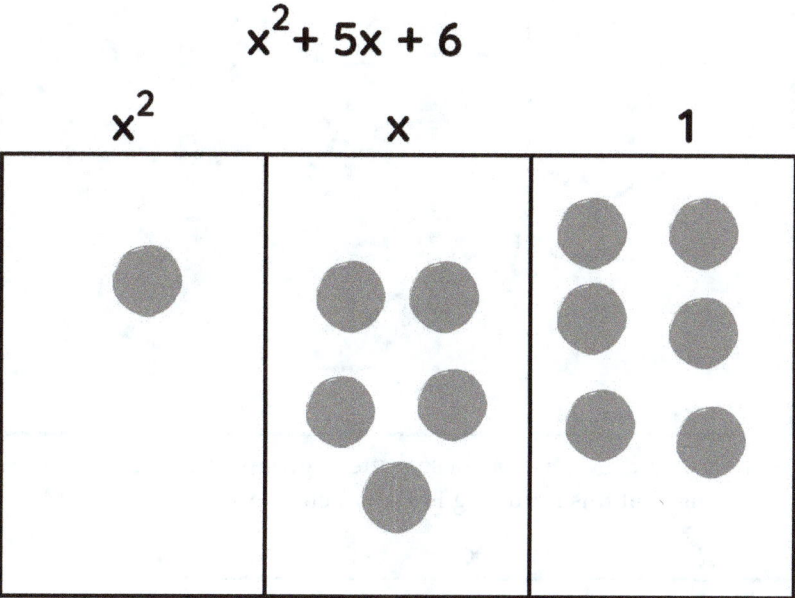

- Explain that the goal is to find pairs of factors that combine to give the original expression. For the example $x^2 + 5x + 6$, guide your learner through the process of identifying which pairs of factors of 6 add up to 5, using the dots to visualize how the factors group together. 6 factors into 2x3 or 6x1. Maybe wonder out loud that it's possible groups of 2 or 3 might be a good place to start when making a pattern.

3. Step-by-Step Visual Breakdown:
- Ask them to try and find a pattern they can group up so that they don't have any left over. I highly recommend a short look at Exploding dots familiarize yourself with this visual method. The basic idea is to try and lasso from one box to an adjacent box and find a dot grouping you can replicate equally. Below I figure out that I can equally separate my dots equally with the pattern of one dot from a left box and 3 from its neighbor.

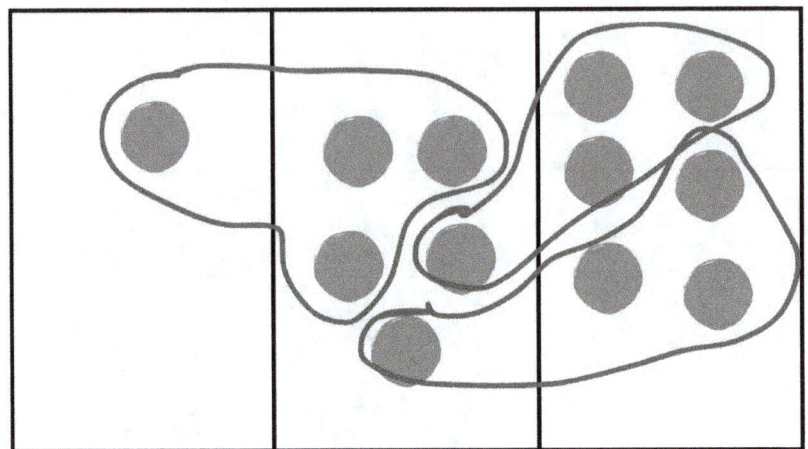

- If you drew one of these pattern groups on its own, you will find that this grouping is equivalent to x+3

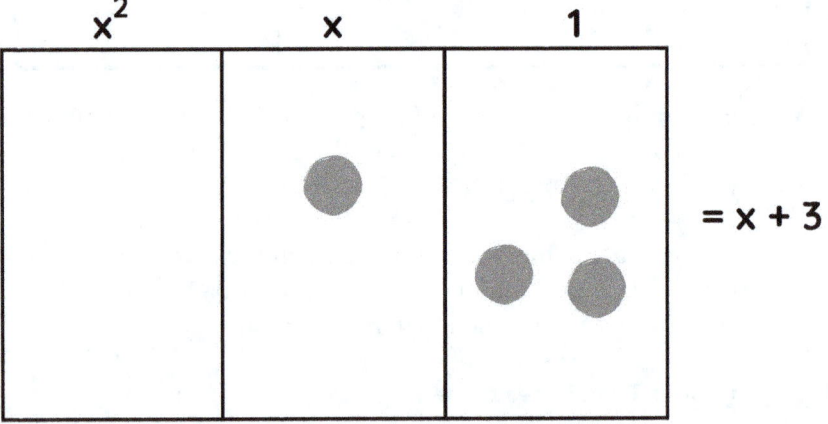

$$x^2 \qquad x \qquad 1$$

$$= x + 3$$

Pattern of 1 -> 3 is a match of x+3

- Now we know that one factor is x+3. Back to the original grouping, you then use the right hand box that each grouping ends in and put a tally mark at the top of the column to find the next factor. In this case, we have 1 tally mark over the "x" column for the blue colored pattern grouping and 2 over the "1" column for the green colored pattern groupings.

* * *

100

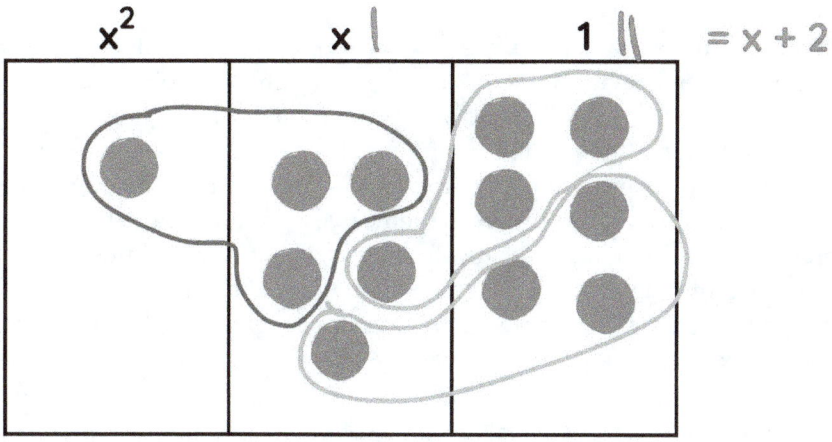

x^2 x | 1 || $= x + 2$

- With 1 tally mark over the "x" column and 2 marks over the "1" column, we know the other factor is x+2.
- Work back through the problem above but start with circling the pattern below to see if you can come up with the same factors.

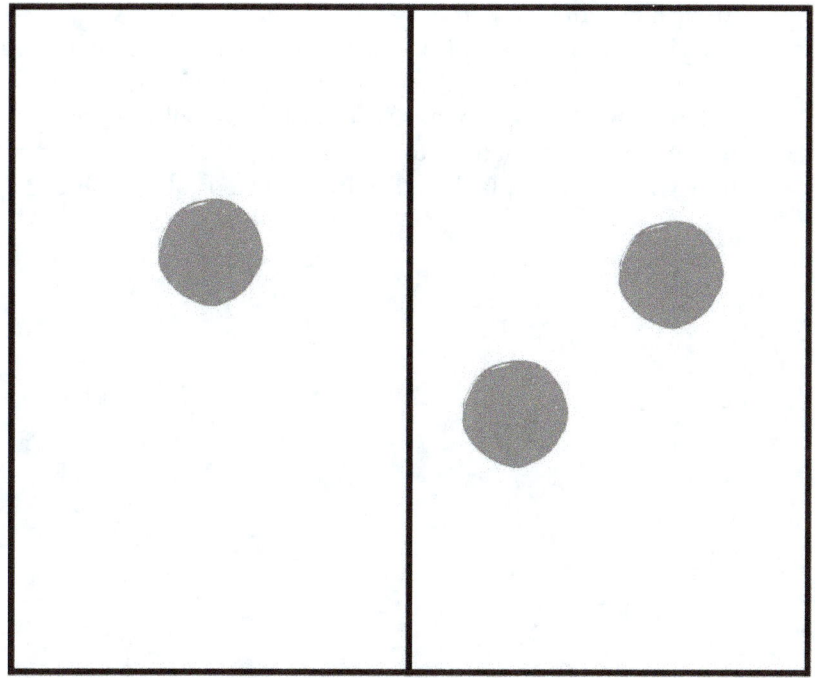

* * *

You have just shown visually shown how the polynomial $x^2 + 5x + 6$ can be broken down into $(x + 2)(x + 3)$! Use different colors or shapes to represent the different factors and highlight how these factors combine to form the original polynomial. This helps your learner see the connections between the components more clearly. Encourage your learner to draw the process themselves, reinforcing the visual breakdown by having them create their own set of exploding dots to represent the factors. You can use a physical sheet to draw out the problem or there are some interactive tools linked in the Resource Appendix.

4. Practice and Reinforcement:
- Provide additional practice problems for your learner to solve using the Exploding Dots technique. Start with polynomials that have simple factors, gradually increasing the complexity as your learner becomes more comfortable with the process. As you become more comfortable, you can expand into using negative numbers. Think of different colored counters representing the (+) elements and the (-) elements and the groupings work the same.
- To reinforce the concept, use a mix of visual tools: have your learner create mind maps that link different types of polynomials to their factors, use flashcards with polynomials on one side and their factored forms on the other, and draw flow charts that guide them through the steps of factoring.

* * *

Polynomial Fraction	Divisor	1 <- X Machine	Quotient
$\dfrac{3x^2 + 10x + 8}{x + 2}$			$3x + 4$
$\dfrac{2x^2 + 7x + 6}{x + 2}$			$2x +$
$\dfrac{2x^2 + 9x + 9}{x + 3}$			
$\dfrac{4x^2 + 14x + 6}{x + 3}$			
$\dfrac{2x^2 + 9x + 10}{2x + 5}$			
$\dfrac{2x^3 + 7x^2 + 8x + 4}{x + 2}$			

Practicing Factoring with Exploding Dots [ref5]

* * *

5 https://startingpointsmaths.com/wp-content/uploads/2020/11/polynomial-division.pdf

5. Creating Memory Aids and Mnemonics:

- Create a mnemonic or visual memory aid to help your learner remember the steps of polynomial factoring. For example, if your learner is factoring a trinomial of the form $x^2 + bx + c$, you could create a mnemonic that links the process to a memorable phrase, such as "Find pairs that multiply to C, but add to B."
- Encourage your learner to visualize this process by drawing a cartoon or simple diagram that illustrates the mnemonic. This can be turned into a flashcard or included in a review binder for regular practice.

6. Connecting to Real-World Examples:

- Help your learner see the relevance of polynomial factoring by connecting it to real-world examples. For instance, explain how factoring can be used to solve problems in physics, engineering, or finance. If possible, find or create a word problem that involves a real-life scenario where polynomial factoring is necessary to find a solution.
- You might also take this opportunity to explore how these concepts are used in higher-level mathematics or different professions, giving your learner a broader context for why understanding polynomial factoring is important.

7. Review and Goal Setting:

- After working through several examples and practice problems, review what your learner has learned. Use mind maps or graphic organizers to summarize the steps involved in polynomial factoring, and ensure they have a clear understanding of the key concepts.
- Set specific, achievable goals for future practice. For example, if your learner struggles with certain types of polynomials, set a goal to focus on those in upcoming lessons. Use visual reminders, such as a checklist or progress chart, to track their achievements. This will really emphasize how much progress has been made instead of focusing on how much work is ahead.

8. Integrating Different Instruction Methods:

- Integrate different visual and interactive methods to reinforce

the learning. For example, use an online interactive algebra app that allows your learner to manipulate and factor polynomials in a visual format, or find a video tutorial that walks through the Exploding Dots technique.
- Use these resources to complement the hands-on practice and help solidify your learner's understanding.

By using visual math techniques like Exploding Dots, you can turn a potentially daunting topic like polynomial factoring into an accessible and engaging learning experience. These strategies help break down complex concepts into simpler, more manageable parts, allowing your learner to see the relationships between different elements of a polynomial. With practice, visual aids, and creative memory tools, your learner can develop a deep understanding of polynomial factoring, building both their skills and confidence in math.

As with any learning process, the key is to tailor the approach to the needs of you learner and their interests, making sure that the material is presented in a way that is both comprehensible and enjoyable. By incorporating these visual techniques, you're not just teaching your learner how to factor polynomials—you're also giving them the tools to approach future math challenges with confidence and curiosity.

CONCLUSION

Visual math strategies can transform your learner's experience with this essential subject, making it more accessible, understandable, and enjoyable. By understanding the neuroscience behind visual learning and implementing general techniques, you can help your child build a strong foundation in math. This foundation not only improves their mathematical skills but also enhances their overall confidence and engagement in learning.

In the next chapter, we will explore how to teach science through visual learning, providing practical tips and techniques to make scientific concepts come alive for your learner.

CHAPTER SIX

Science Through Pictures: Exploring the Natural World Visually

INTRODUCTION

Science is a subject brimming with wonder and discovery, offering endless opportunities for exploration and curiosity. For neurodivergent children, visual learning can make the study of science even more captivating and accessible. Visual models, in particular, play a crucial role in helping learners conceptualize and understand complex processes that are not easily observable. These models allow learners to engage with scientific concepts in a tangible way, making abstract ideas more concrete and understandable.

Visual learning techniques tap into the brain's natural ability to process visual information, enhancing comprehension and retention. Mental models, which are learners' pre-existing conceptual understandings of a process, directly inform how they create and interpret visual models. For example, when studying DNA, a learner might start with a concrete physical model, such as a DNA helix constructed from a model kit. This physical representation helps solidify the mental image of the DNA structure. As the guide introduces a verbal model, describing DNA as a twisted ladder with sugar-phosphate backbones as the rails and base pairs as the rungs, the learner's mental model evolves to incorporate this new information. The use of symbolic models, like analyzing the percentage composition of base pairs if, for example, 20% of your structure is "C" and figuring out with simple ratios that therefore "A" must be 30% of the structure, further refines the learner's understanding by introducing abstract concepts into the visual model. Finally, animations and gestural models, such as mimicking the zipping and unzipping of DNA with a zipper or by interlocking your fingers, help learners visualize dynamic processes in a way that static models cannot. Through these iterative steps, learners update their mental models, making them more accurate and reflective of the underlying scientific reality. [BRYCE[6]]

In this chapter, we will explore general techniques for teaching science through visual methods, delve into the neuroscience behind why these techniques are so effective, and demonstrate how visual learning can deepen scientific understanding. By integrating these strategies into your homeschool curriculum, you can ignite a passion for science in your learner, making the study of the natural world a dynamic and engaging experience.

PERSONAL STORIES: VISUAL SCIENCE SUCCESS

Liam's Experiential Learning as a Homeschooler

Liam, a nine-year-old with autism, struggled with traditional science classes. The abstract concepts, overwhelming sensory input, and rigid structure made it difficult for him to focus and engage, often leading to frustration and refusal to participate. Recognizing that he needed a different approach, his parents decided to homeschool him, with a focus on visual and experiential science learning. This decision marked the beginning of a transformative journey that not only deepened Liam's understanding of science but also ignited a passion for discovery.

Hands-On Experiments and Visual Learning

---

[6] BRYCE, CALEB M., et al. "Exploring Models in the Biology Classroom." *The American Biology Teacher*, vol. 78, no. 1, 2016, pp. 35–42. *JSTOR*, https://www.jstor.org/stable/26410992. Accessed 6 Aug. 2024

* * *

Liam's parents knew that traditional textbooks wouldn't capture his interest, so they turned to hands-on experiments that allowed him to see and experience science in action. Each week, they conducted experiments that made scientific concepts tangible. For example, when learning about geological processes, they built a volcano model together. Liam eagerly mixed baking soda and vinegar, watching in awe as the "lava" erupted from the volcano. This experiment didn't just teach him about chemical reactions; it also provided a memorable visual and tactile experience that solidified his understanding of natural phenomena.

To explore biology, Liam's parents introduced 3D models of the human body. They used these models to explain how different organs function, allowing Liam to physically manipulate the parts and see how they fit together. This hands-on approach made the complex workings of the body more accessible, helping Liam visualize and grasp concepts that would have otherwise seemed abstract and overwhelming.

Field Trips and Real-World Exploration

Understanding that Liam thrived in natural settings, his parents incorporated regular field trips into their science curriculum. They visited nature reserves, where Liam could observe wildlife in its natural habitat. During these trips, he learned about ecosystems, animal behavior, and plant life, all while being immersed in the environment. One of his favorite activities was bird watching, where he used binoculars to spot different species, excitedly identifying them with the help of a field guide.

They also took advantage of local resources by joining a homeschool course run by their science museum, led by a Master Naturalist. This course brought science to life through guided explorations of nearby parks and natural areas. Liam met other learners in these settings, where they searched for fossils, studied plant life, and learned about the local ecosystem. These experiences not only enriched his understanding of science but also helped him develop social skills and make connections with peers who shared his interests.

* * *

108

Collaborative Learning and Community Engagement

In addition to field trips, Liam's family joined a Barefoot University group, a community of homeschoolers who meet weekly to explore the natural world. Each session involved a different project, such as building shelters with natural materials or mapping out a forested area. These collaborative activities allowed Liam to engage with others in a low-pressure, supportive environment. He loved the hands-on aspect of these projects and took pride in contributing to the group's creations.

The impact of these experiences was profound. Science, once a source of anxiety, became Liam's favorite subject. He began to open up socially, eagerly sharing his discoveries with others. He even claimed a special shelf in his learning space to display his growing fossil collection, which he proudly showed to anyone who visited.

The Transformation

Liam's transformation through visual and experiential science learning was remarkable. What started as an effort to make science more accessible for him turned into a journey of exploration and personal growth. By tailoring his education to his unique needs, his parents not only helped him develop a deep understanding of scientific concepts but also fostered his natural curiosity and love for learning.

Through this approach, Liam's parents were able to create a learning environment where he could thrive, both academically and socially. Science became more than just a subject for Liam; it became a gateway to understanding the world around him and a source of endless fascination. His story is a testament to the power of experiential learning and the importance of adapting education to meet the individual needs of every learner.

GENERAL TECHNIQUES FOR VISUAL SCIENCE LEARNING

Think back to your time in school and to what science memories you have from your elementary or middle school days. It's likely the things you remember were when something exploded, changed colors or seemed like magic made real. For high school it might be the egg you dropped from the roof or the bridge model you built with popsicle sticks and collapsed with textbooks as weights. It would be unusual to still remember the finer points of a particular lecture or what topics were even covered in those courses, especially when the material is presented in a pure lecture format or in a way where you only needed to retain it for a test as you were likely prioritizing you time for things that interested you more.

Science is magic made real! It helps us explain and understand the world that we live in. Historically, the sciences were always a course of discovery and natural curiosity about the world would lead early scientists to make models, test the model and revise the model if one of its assumptions was provided wrong. Traditional classroom science course are adapted forms to form fit a prescribed course of study regardless of interest that is condensed and summarized so it can be fed to 35 kids inside a windowless room via worksheets and the occasional video within a 45 minute time period. With homeschooling you can instead refocus on allowing curiosity to drive your discoveries. You can make science engaging in ways that make the concepts stick long-term and in ways that encourage critical thinking instead of the short-term retention that's gained from traditional lecture/worksheet methods. We will work to provide you the structure you need so that your science classes can include fewer worksheets and more:

- **Experiments and Demonstrations:** Conducting hands-on experiments and demonstrations, visualizing chemical reactions, physical phenomena, or biological processes helps learners grasp complex concepts.
- **Diagrams and Models**: The use of diagrams and models to illustrate scientific ideas makes more abstract concepts more tangible. For example, 3D models of the solar system or the human body are tactile and allow your learner to explore a lesson in a hands-on way.
- **Videos and Animations**: We will leverage educational videos and animations to show processes that are difficult to observe directly, such as cellular functions or geological formations. A picture is worth 1,000 words and a video of cellular digestion is worth a chapter of content and doesn't use up your learner's

110

verbal processing buffer.

- **Field Trips and Nature Walks**: We will take learning outside the home with field trips to science museums, botanical gardens, or nature reserves. Observing nature firsthand enhances understanding and retention. Even if you will need to accompany your learner as a hands-on-aide, don't discount the impact these experiences can have.

- **Interactive Simulations**: We will use interactive simulations and virtual labs to explore scientific concepts. These tools allow your learner to experiment and learn in a controlled, risk-free environment. It's much less messy to practice that chemistry experiment in a virtual lab before doing it for real. I'll also share resources that will allow you to dive into 3-D molecular models with equipment as simple as a smart phone.

* * *

Science courses can seem challenging to adapt for a neurodiverse learner. Public schools in particular seem to struggle in breaking down concepts or adapting the curriculum in ways that don't overtax visual processing, verbal processing or adjust for social deficiencies. Common characteristics among neurodiverse learners when engaging with science concepts are similar to other subjects and they may have deficits in processing skills, memory, language, and/or attention. [Steele, 2007[7]]

Common Challenges for a Neurodiverse Learner when Learning Science Topics:

Auditory Processing Problems

Students with learning disabilities (LD), Attention Deficit Hyperactivity Disorder (ADHD), and Communication Disorders (CD) often face significant challenges in understanding science information presented in a lecture format or during class discussions. These students may struggle to process spoken information effectively, particularly when it involves complex or multi-step instructions. As a result, following along in real-time can become confusing and overwhelming, leading to gaps in comprehension and difficulty keeping up with the lesson.

Motor Skill Deficiencies

For students with motor skill deficiencies or motor processing issues, hands-on activities in science, such as handling chemicals or conducting experiments, can pose safety risks. Their difficulties in coordinating fine motor skills can make precise actions, like measuring substances or assembling equipment, challenging. This not only impacts their ability to participate fully in lab activities but also raises concerns about their safety in a science classroom setting.

Memory and Information Retention

---

[7] Steele, Marcee. "TEACHING SCIENCE to STUDENTS with LEARNING DIFFERENCES: Strategies to Create Positive Experiences for Students with Learning Problems in High School Biology, Earth Science, and Chemistry Classes." *The Science Teacher*, vol. 74, no. 3, 2007, pp. 24–27. *JSTOR*, http://www.jstor.org/stable/24141371. Accessed 6 Aug. 2024.

Retaining new information and recalling previously learned concepts can be particularly challenging for students with certain neurodivergent conditions. These memory issues can hinder their ability to build upon foundational knowledge, making it difficult to progress through more complex scientific topics. The struggle to retain and recall information can also affect their confidence and motivation in the subject.

Expressive Language Problems

Students who experience expressive language problems may find it difficult to discuss scientific procedures, results, and conclusions with their peers. These challenges can extend to making presentations and effectively communicating their understanding of scientific concepts. Their difficulties with verbal expression can lead to frustration and may hinder their ability to participate fully in group work or class discussions, impacting their overall learning experience.

As with all subjects, I will introduce some techniques for adapting your curriculum for your learner at whatever level you are at. Similar to the mathematics chapter, I will not employ grade-level assignment to subjects as part of the joy and flexibility of homeschooling allows you to delve into material as deep as your student may be interested in it. For example, I have a "high-school" aged learner that still believes in Santa Claus. This does not prevent him from wanting to sing about the elemental components of glucose at age 10 or limit his capability to construct biochemical models of glucose at age 12. Our learners are varied in both their capabilities and their needs. The idea is to take these adaptations for learning science topics and apply them systematically and with an overall goal in mind.

- Don't be afraid to introduce some of the more "complicated" vocabulary words to your younger learners. This makes those phrases not so new when they are reused at a later date with more detail behind them.
- Work with your learner to set specific, achievable science goals. Buy-in and ownership of the goals is key to giving your learner a sense of control. You can use a goal breakdown sheet (see example of one in Chapter 2) to help them see and work through how you can break down a larger goal into achievable mini-goals or tasks. Taking on a large goal all at once can tax a

learner's executive function leading to a hesitancy to get starting or task paralysis. Helping your learner break down a larger project, task or goal is an excellent life skill concept that will provide them with a tool that they can later use independently.

- Regularly review and adjust goals based on progress and feedback. Having a visual of progress made towards a goal helps with executive function by approaching a larger objective piece by piece. Regular review and progress tracking will help keep you and your learner on track.

Visual learning can make advanced science concepts exciting and comprehensible for your learner. You can explore simulations and virtual labs to explore scientific concepts that are difficult to observe directly. You can conduct experiments that have clear visual outcomes, such as chemical reactions with a color change or physical demonstrations. For each concept, try and think of a way to model it with a 3-D model. There are many inexpensive science kits that are available for purchase for constructing molecules, for example, or you can create your own versions with toothpicks and modeling clay or materials as simple as colored paper to construct a DNA model. You can use Play-Dough to make organs or components of a cell and get some sensory inputs in your day as well! You can also utilize virtual reality (VR) tools (see the resource Appendix for specific VR Resources) to explore scientific concepts. These technologies can help students visualize processes, structures, and phenomena in an immersive way. If you can augment and meld multiple modes of exploring a concept will help to cement the ideas for your learner.

* * *

VR-Simulation of a Chemical Reaction

Work with your learner to represent data or concepts visually with charts, graphs, and infographics. This will help them interpret and communicate scientific findings more effectively. We will also explore the utilization of mnemonics as another great technique that can help learners that struggle with processing complex ideas. By constructing a rhyme, song or sentence where the first letter of each sentence is the element involved in a particular process, you can curb frustration with new or complex topics. Finally, find a real-world connection to the concept you are learning. Encourage field research or find virtual tours of scientific sites, research facilities, and natural environments. These experiences provide real-world context and enhance understanding.

* * *

Here are some general strategies and modifications you can employ when introducing a new science concept:

- **Memory Aids:** Use mnemonics, picture cues, keywords, association clues, and acronyms to assist with recall of content.
- **Visual Displays**: Introduce and organize new and challenging information using flow charts, outlines, and graphic organizers. Utilize illustrations and animations to clarify complex topics.
- **Goal Setting**: Assist your learner in setting appropriate science goals. Buy-in and ownership of the goals are key to giving your learner a sense of control.
- **Varied Methods of Instruction:** Integrate visual demonstrations, animations, videos, and virtual simulations into learning each concept.
- **Vocabulary Support**: Generate keyword cards for vocabulary concepts your student is struggling with. Create cartoons or funny ways to remember what the word means or how to pronounce it. Review vocabulary keyword cards from prior lessons before introducing new topics.
- **Graphic Organizers:** Use graphic organizers or visual displays to introduce and highlight key ideas.
- **Relate to Real-World Themes**: Relate science concepts to real-world themes or examples of change, ecology, or equilibrium to help with focus and prevent frustration with overwhelming detail.

THE NEUROSCIENCE BEHIND VISUAL LEARNING IN SCIENCE

The effectiveness of visual learning in science education is rooted in how the brain processes and retains information:

1. **Visual-Spatial Processing**: The brain's visual-spatial processing abilities allow it to interpret and remember images more easily than text. This makes diagrams, models, and animations powerful tools for understanding scientific concepts.

2.   **Multisensory Learning**: Engaging multiple senses strengthens learning. Visual learning combined with hands-on activities or auditory explanations creates a richer learning experience, enhancing memory and understanding.

3.   **Pattern Recognition**: The brain excels at recognizing patterns, which is crucial in science. Visual aids can highlight patterns in data, biological systems, or physical laws, aiding comprehension.

HOW VISUAL LEARNING ENHANCES SCIENCE OUTCOMES FOR NEURODIVERGENT LEARNERS

Visual learning not only makes science more accessible for neurodivergent learners but also deepens their overall understanding in several key ways:

- **Concrete Visualization of Abstract Concepts**: Visual tools provide a tangible way to grasp abstract scientific concepts. For example, using a visual model of DNA allows learners to better understand its structure and function. Constructing physical models with household items can further break down these concepts into manageable parts, with the added benefit of customizing colors, shapes, and sizes to enhance understanding of specific ideas.

- **Enhanced Inquiry and Exploration**: Visual learning naturally fosters curiosity and a desire to explore. When learners can visually see the results of experiments or the intricacies of natural phenomena, they are more likely to engage in deeper inquiry and ask more questions about the world around them.

- **Improved Retention and Recall:** Visual representations significantly aid in memory retention. Learners are more likely to remember scientific processes and concepts when they can visualize them. For optimal retention and recall, constructing visual aids together can be highly effective. Referencing online visuals as a guide, then recreating these visuals by hand, allows you and your learner to highlight important concepts, simplify complex ideas, and adapt language to match your learner's reading level. This collaborative process makes the material more meaningful and easier to recall.

- **Increased Engagement and Motivation**: Visual learning makes science more engaging and enjoyable. Engaging visuals and interactive activities capture a learner's attention, making them more motivated to explore and learn.

In my homeschool, visuals often take the form of comics, tapping into my learner's special interest in that format. For example, when learning about cell mitosis, we might create a comic strip that personifies the different stages of mitosis—prophase, metaphase, anaphase, and telophase—into characters on a journey. Each stage is represented by a different character, navigating through the steps of cell division. This creative approach helps break down the complex process of mitosis into smaller, more manageable parts that are easier to understand and remember. You don't need to be a skilled artist to create effective visuals; even simple stick figures can make learning fun and accessible. The comic format allows for a visual and narrative exploration of scientific processes, making the material engaging and relatable for learners.

* * *

Comics are a fun way to break down an idea

IMPLEMENTING VISUAL SCIENCE LEARNING

Let's work through these strategies with an example for learning the concept of photosynthesis. You can expand, eliminate or simplify any step to bring it to a level appropriate for your learner. When first introducing the topic for an early learner, it may just involve sprouting some seeds in a sunny window and talking about how the leaves take in sunshine and water and the plant makes its own food. For older learners or learners that express more interest, you can go as deeply into the topic as your resources allow. Take a trip to the library and find non-fiction resources in a format that speaks to your learner. It could be an early-reader or a graphic novel. You may be surprised at the variety of printed materials and resources your librarian can help you find at no cost to you. Don't shy away from "college level" vocabulary just because your learner is 12 especially if they are expressing a particular interest in the topic. At the same time, if your learner is expressing anxiety or difficulty in retaining or understanding material, you can simplify it or find a way to customize it in the specific ways they enjoy learning.

Photosynthesis Example Lesson Plan:

First, I'd look up some graphic organizers and use them to describe the process in general. If there was any new vocabulary, or if my learner indicated confusion of any words or compounds, I'd grab an index card and write that specific item down and either define it or draw a simple cartoon to provide it more context. Next I would draw a visual representation of the process of photosynthesis. As each keyword is reintroduced, pull out that keyword or concept card or make additional ones as needed. By using a simple one like the one below, you can annotate with keywords as you walk through the process or you can leave it blank and have a "Quiz Show" game where you can say a keyword and your learner can point to the visual representation.

Annotate visuals with sticker labels

You don't have to be a great artist as there are lots of examples you can

120

pick up online. I do suggest only using what you find as a reference for you, the guide, and then either annotation a simple graphic like the one above to reconstructing a more complex visual by hand, piece by piece, using colored markers or with your learner on a whiteboard so you introduce each step of the process at their pace and not overwhelm them with too much information at once. As you get into the higher level concepts for the chemical process, you can employ other methods like constructing a mnemonic. The equation for photosynthesis is often expected for public high school students to memorize but your learner may balk when presented with the equation:

$$6CO_2 + 6H_2O + light \longrightarrow C_6H_{12}O_6 + 6O_2$$

Let's take it apart by starting with the first letter of each of the steps:
- C: Carbon Dioxide (CO_2)
- W: Water (H_2O)
- S: Sunlight (Daylight)
- G: Glucose ($C_6H_{12}O_6$)
- O: Oxygen (O_2)

Now we can create a silly sentence like, "Can Whales Slurp Green Oranges?". This mnemonic can also be drawn as a graphic with colored markers on a key concept card and put into your review pile.

* * *

Photosynthesis Mneumonic: Can Whales Slurp Green Oranges?

It's a fun way to represent the simplified process of photosynthesis and can help trigger your learner's memory by breaking it up into smaller pieces so they don't have to recall the entire thing at once, just one letter at a time. First, have your learner say the sentence, then write down the first letters of the sentence in a line like so:

1. C
2. W
3. S
4. G
5. O

Now, one at a time, they can fill out as much information as they remember. By only focusing on one letter at a time, you can reduce

122

some of the processing load with recall from memory.

1. Carbon Dioxide (CO_2)
2. Water (H_2O)
3. Sunlight (Daylight)
4. Glucose ($C_6H_{12}O_6$)
5. Oxygen (O_2)

Finally, ask your learner to annotate, describe, act out, or draw what each piece is doing in the process. For example:

1. Carbon Dioxide (CO_2): Enters the plant through small openings called stomata.
2. Water (H_2O): Absorbed by the plant roots from the soil.
3. Sunlight (Daylight): Captured by chlorophyll in the chloroplasts.
4. Glucose ($C_6H_{12}O_6$): Produced as a form of sugar that serves as food for the plant.
5. Oxygen (O_2): Released as a byproduct into the atmosphere.

There are also some fantastic songs to help with both understanding and with remembering the steps in photosynthesis you can access on resources like YouTube. This one from MosaMack[8] is particularly catchy:

"Give me 6 water, 6 carbon dioxide, I take that and look what I do on the inside!
With light as my engine, I can't wait to taste… the glucose I make.
Give 6 oxygen as waste."

After snapping your fingers to the tune of that song, it might become an ear worm that you or your learner remembers a little *too* well. As a homeschooler, you are not restricted to worksheets and classrooms, take a nature walk, visit a local park or wander your yard or neighborhood to make observations about some plants outside. I'd observe the color and the angle of the leaves to the sun. You can point out when parts of the photosynthesis cycle happen everyday. For

---

[8] https://youtu.be/uYksRZebxic

example, as the plant is busy making glucose, it's less able to work on absorbing water from its roots. At night, it will restore its water supply. You can then explain why that makes it more efficient to water your plants after the sun has gone down. Bringing up related concepts related to water conservation including why watering at night leads to less water waste due to evaporation, etc., can also help link real-world decisions you make for your garden or flower bed relate directly to the chemistry behind photosynthesis. Finally, employ some more open ended critical thinking questions by asking your learner how they think a plant may be affected by air or water pollution. What would the plant might look like could be written, spoken or demonstrated by acting it out, drawing a cartoon or pointing to an example outside. Finally, create simple experiments by sprouting several seeds in containers and then exposing them to different conditions like dark vs light or too much water vs not enough. Make a chart and revisit your sprouts each day and record your observations. You can even "pollute" the soil of a healthy plant with several drops of white vinegar and observe what happens to your plant over time. This concept is not something you might present all in one day. Break it up as it suits your needs. Keep your keyword and key concepts cards handy and review them before starting into new or related material. These are portable and we often use them when on the road or to review before dinner. This technique can helps students that struggle with working memory and concept retention.

Sometimes when introducing a new concept, I will see how it is taken in before working up several different aids and models. If my learner seems to understand the concept and there is more interest in moving on, we will go to the next topic. If my learner shows some struggles in learning, I will slow down and revisit the topic with additional visual models until I find a good fit for my learner. If my learner shows great interest and excitement, I might do the same thing so that he can delve as deeply into the topic as he likes. In general when preparing a science lesson for your learner, create a targeted toolkit of visual aids and strategies tailored to the concept you will introduce and to your learner's interests and needs:

- Gather Materials:
    - Whiteboard and markers
    - Flashcards and index cards

124

- Poster board for graphic organizers and print-outs of visual aids
- Links to related educational videos and animations
- Tools for creating mnemonics and visual cues (e.g., colored pencils, drawing software)
- Develop Memory Aids:
  - Work with your learner to create mnemonics for key concepts.
  - Design flashcards with keywords and concept illustrations to aid memory.
- Create Visual Displays:
  - Construct flow charts and graphic organizers for complex processes with your learner.
  - Use animations and videos to illustrate scientific concepts.
- Set and Review Goals:
  - Help your learner set specific, achievable science goals.
  - Regularly review and adjust goals based on progress and feedback.
- Integrate Various Instruction Methods:
  - Plan lessons that incorporate visual demonstrations and virtual simulations.
  - Use real-world examples to make abstract concepts more relatable and engaging.

By using these strategies and modifications, you can create an effective and supportive learning environment that accommodates the unique needs of your neurodivergent scientist. This approach adapts material to address common classroom struggles for neurodivergent learners, helps learners to understand scientific concepts and also fosters a positive and engaging learning experience.

CONCLUSION

Visual science learning can make this fascinating subject even more accessible and enjoyable for neurodivergent children. By understanding the neuroscience behind visual learning and implementing effective techniques, you can help your child build a deep, lasting understanding of scientific concepts. This approach not only enhances their scientific knowledge but also fosters a lifelong curiosity and love for learning.

In the next chapter, we will explore how to teach the humanities through visual learning, providing practical tips and techniques to make reading an engaging and effective experience for your child.

CHAPTER SEVEN

The Humanities Visually: Stories, Comprehension, and Beyond

INTRODUCTION

The humanities encompass a wide range of subjects, including literature, social studies, history, writing, and related disciplines. These areas are interconnected, each providing a different lens through which learners can explore and understand the world. For neurodivergent learners, traditional methods of studying the humanities can present challenges. Not only are they disconnected from one another in a traditional school setting, but they generally rely on modes of gauging understanding that don't align with how neurodivergent learners organize information or leans on skills like writing or speaking that may be a struggle for learners with processing differences. Visual learning strategies offer an engaging and comprehensible approach, making these subjects more accessible and enjoyable. [Renino[9]]

In homeschooling, it's common to integrate the humanities in a variety of ways rather than focusing on them individually. For example, non-fiction novels that focus on historical events or historical fiction can

---

[9] Renino, Christopher. "'Who's There?': Shakespeare and the Dragon of Autism." *The English Journal*, vol. 99, no. 1, 2009, pp. 50–55. *JSTOR*, http://www.jstor.org/stable/40503326. Accessed 6 Aug. 2024.

serve multiple educational purposes, blending literature with social studies and history. Visual models play a critical role in understanding historical contexts and the development of knowledge over time. For instance, when studying navigational maps used before modern technology, learners can compare these early maps with current ones to evaluate the accuracy and limitations of historical models. This exercise not only helps learners understand the historical context but also teaches them to critically assess how these models evolved as new information became available.

Similarly, Leonardo da Vinci's Vitruvian Man, beyond its cultural and historical significance, serves as a model of human proportions that can be analyzed and tested. Learners can take measurements of family members and compare them to da Vinci's ideal proportions, creating scatterplots to visualize the data. This activity not only brings history to life but also helps learners understand the assumptions and limitations of historical models. If a learner struggles with this inquiry, the guide can pose the questions aloud and work through the process together, aiding the learner in understanding the model's assumptions and developing new models based on their findings. [Bryce[10]]

This chapter will explore general techniques for teaching the humanities through visual methods, delve into the neuroscience behind why these techniques are effective, and demonstrate how visual learning enhances comprehension and enjoyment in subjects that are foundational to a well-rounded education.

PERSONAL STORIES: VISUAL READING SUCCESS

Sophia, an eight-year-old with ADHD, struggled with traditional reading methods and often lost interest quickly, making it difficult for her to engage with the material. Recognizing the need for a different approach as she was falling behind the skills levels needed to progress to more complex topics, her parents decided to incorporate visual

---

[10] BRYCE, CALEB M., et al. "Exploring Models in the Biology Classroom." *The American Biology Teacher*, vol. 78, no. 1, 2016, pp. 35–42. *JSTOR*, https://www.jstor.org/stable/26410992. Accessed 6 Aug. 2024.

128

strategies into her homeschooling curriculum, particularly in the humanities. By integrating visual learning tools across history, social studies, and literature, they were able to make these subjects more accessible and enjoyable for Sophia.

Literature: Engaging with Stories Through Graphic Novels

Sophia initially found it hard to stay focused on lengthy texts, so her parents introduced her to graphic novels. The combination of text and illustrations helped her follow the story more easily, as the visuals provided context and kept her engaged.

Example - Reading "Charlotte's Web":
- **Graphic Novel Adaptation:** Instead of reading the full text of Charlotte's Web, Sophia read a graphic novel adaptation. The vivid illustrations helped her visualize the characters and the farm setting, making the story come to life in a way that plain text couldn't.
- **Visual Storyboarding**: After reading a chapter, Sophia created a storyboard summarizing the key events. For example, she drew scenes depicting Wilbur's adventures and Charlotte's web designs, reinforcing her understanding of the plot and character relationships.
- **Character Flashcards:** To help with vocabulary and character recognition, her parents made flashcards with images of each character alongside their names and a brief description. This visual reinforcement helped Sophia remember the details more effectively.

History: Bringing Historical Events to Life

Sophia's parents knew that she needed a more dynamic way to engage with history, so they used visual aids and interactive tools to make the past come alive.

Example - Learning About Ancient Egypt:
- **Picture Books and Timelines**: To introduce Sophia to Ancient Egypt, her parents used richly illustrated picture books that depicted the daily life of Egyptians, their gods, and their pyramids. They also created a visual timeline, placing key

events such as the construction of the Pyramids of Giza and the reign of King Tutankhamun on a large poster that Sophia could refer to.

- **Hands-On Projects**: Sophia built a simple model of a pyramid using clay, which helped her understand the structure and significance of these ancient monuments. This tactile activity reinforced her learning and provided a sense of accomplishment.
- **Interactive History Apps:** Her parents also introduced Sophia to an interactive app where she could explore a virtual Ancient Egyptian world, walking through temples and seeing hieroglyphics come to life. This immersive experience kept her engaged and made the historical content more relatable.
- **Digital Tools:** The Smithsonian website for the National Museum of Natural History provides virtual access to the Smithsonian's' collection of Egyptian artifacts. Sofia created trading cards for her favorite artifacts and used them to create a storytelling game about Ancient Egypt.

Social Studies: Understanding Community and Government Through Visual Tools

In social studies, Sophia's parents used visual learning strategies to help her grasp complex concepts like community roles and government structures.

Example - Exploring Community Roles:
- Community Map Creation: Sophia and her parents created a large, colorful map of their town, marking important places like the fire station, library, and grocery store. They used stickers to represent different community helpers, such as firefighters, librarians, and cashiers. This map helped Sophia understand the roles these people play in her community.
- Role-Playing with Puppets: To further explore the concept of community roles, Sophia used puppets to act out scenarios, such as a firefighter rescuing someone or a librarian helping a child find a book. This role-playing allowed her to visualize and internalize the information in a fun and interactive way.
- Mind Mapping Government Concepts: When learning about local government, Sophia's parents used mind maps to break

130

down the roles of different government officials. They created a visual diagram showing the mayor, city council, and various departments, helping Sophia see how each part of the government works together to serve the community.

Through the integration of visual learning tools across literature, history, and social studies, Sophia's experience with the humanities was transformed. What once felt challenging and disengaging became a series of enjoyable, interactive learning sessions. Her comprehension and retention improved, and she began to look forward to exploring new stories, historical events, and social concepts. By adapting their homeschooling approach to include visual aids and hands-on activities, Sophia's parents were able to meet her unique learning needs, fostering a love for learning that continues to grow.

GENERAL TECHNIQUES FOR VISUAL READING

Visual learners benefit greatly from seeing text and concepts accompanied by images and other visual aids. When teaching the humanities—encompassing history, social studies, and literature—it's essential to incorporate techniques that make these subjects more accessible and engaging for neurodivergent learners. Here are some key strategies:

- **Picture Books, Graphic Novels, and Illustrated Texts**: Use picture books, graphic novels, and illustrated texts to make humanities topics more engaging. The combination of text and illustrations helps learners understand complex historical events, social concepts, and literary themes, aiding retention and comprehension.
- **Visual Storytelling**: Incorporate visual storytelling techniques, such as storyboards, comic strips, and illustrated timelines. These methods can help learners visualize historical events, social developments, or literary narratives, making it easier for them to follow along and engage with the material.
- **Interactive Learning Tools**: Utilize interactive apps and tools that include animations, highlighted text, and multimedia features. These tools can bring history, social studies, and

literature to life, making learning more dynamic and enjoyable. For example, interactive history apps might show animated battles, while literature apps can highlight key passages and themes.

- **Word Walls, Flashcards, and Visual Vocabulary**: Create word walls and use flashcards with pictures to reinforce key vocabulary and concepts in history, social studies, and literature. Visual aids help learners associate words with images, enhancing memory and recall. For history, you might include images of historical figures or landmarks; for literature, pictures of characters or symbols.

- **Mind Mapping for Comprehension and Analysis:** Use mind maps to break down and analyze complex texts, historical events, or social studies topics. Visualizing the main ideas, key figures, causes and effects, or plot points can help learners organize and understand the material. For example, a mind map might visually outline the causes and consequences of a historical event, the themes in a novel, or the structure of a government system.

These techniques make the humanities more accessible and engaging for neurodivergent learners, helping them connect with and understand the material in a way that aligns with their visual learning style.

THE NEUROSCIENCE BEHIND VISUAL READING

The brain's ability to process visual information plays a crucial role not only in how children learn to read but also in how they comprehend and engage with broader humanities subjects such as history, social studies, and literature. Visual learning techniques tap into this natural processing strength, making complex information more accessible and memorable.

- **Dual Coding Theory**: Dual coding theory suggests that combining visual and verbal information enhances learning and memory. In the context of the humanities, when learners see visual representations (like images, diagrams, or timelines)

132

alongside verbal information (such as text or spoken words), they create stronger neural connections. This dual input helps improve comprehension and retention across subjects like literature, where visual storytelling can deepen understanding, or history, where visual timelines and maps make events more tangible.

- **Visual-Spatial Processing**: The brain's visual-spatial processing abilities allow it to interpret and remember images more easily than text alone. This is why illustrated books, visual timelines, and maps are such powerful tools in the humanities. For instance, visual aids in social studies, like community maps or government charts, help learners better grasp abstract concepts by grounding them in concrete visual representations.

- **Working Memory and Cognitive Load**: Visual aids can significantly reduce cognitive load by breaking down complex information into manageable parts. This is particularly beneficial for learners with working memory challenges, as it allows them to process and retain information more effectively. In the humanities, visual tools like mind maps or graphic organizers can simplify the organization of complex historical events or literary themes, making it easier for learners to understand and recall key information.

These neuroscience principles highlight the importance of incorporating visual learning techniques into teaching the humanities, offering a pathway to deeper comprehension and more meaningful engagement with the material.

HOW VISUAL LEARNING ENHANCES READING COMPREHENSION

Visual learning not only makes subjects like history, social studies, and literature more accessible but also significantly strengthens overall comprehension across the humanities in several key ways:

- **Contextual Understanding:** Visual aids provide critical context for understanding complex historical events, social concepts, and literary narratives. For example, maps, timelines, and illustrations can clarify the setting and sequence of events in history, making it easier for learners to grasp the flow of time and cause-and-effect relationships. In literature, visual representations of characters and settings help learners visualize the story, deepening their connection to the material.

- **Improved Retention and Recall**: Visual representations play a crucial role in memory retention. Learners are more likely to remember key historical events, social structures, and literary themes when these concepts are presented alongside illustrations, diagrams, or graphic organizers. This enhanced retention makes it easier for learners to recall and discuss material during assessments or in-depth discussions.
- **Enhanced Engagement and Motivation**: Visual learning techniques can make the humanities more engaging and enjoyable. For instance, using interactive timelines or creating visual storyboards for literary works captures learners' attention and encourages active participation. This increased engagement often leads to a greater interest in the subject matter and a desire to explore it further.
- **Support for Diverse Learners**: Visual aids offer essential support for learners who struggle with traditional text-based approaches. By providing alternative ways to access and understand complex humanities topics, such as through visual summaries of historical events or graphic novels for literature, visual learning bridges the gap and ensures that all learners can grasp and appreciate the material.

These strategies underscore the significant impact that visual learning has on enhancing comprehension across the humanities, making these subjects more accessible, memorable, and engaging for all learners. In my homeschool, I often use visuals like comics, which align with my learner's special interests, ensuring a higher level of engagement. For instance, we might integrate other interests, such as trains, to guide him through historical concepts by using train tracks as visual aids. The purpose of these visuals is to break down complex topics into smaller, more manageable pieces. You don't need to be an artist to create effective visuals. For example, simple stick figure comics can transport learners back in time to visit the Boston Tea Party as a time traveler, allowing them to explore historical events, ask historical figures questions, and learn about key figures and locations. Additionally, drawing maps or taking virtual field trips to study locations, and even exploring the types of foods or clothing worn during a certain period through online research, can make the learning experience both interactive and immersive.

IMPLEMENTING VISUAL LEARNING TECHNIQUES: THE BOSTON TEA PARTY AND PAUL REVERE'S RIDE

The Boston Tea Party is a pivotal event in American history, offering rich opportunities for a cross-disciplinary study that includes both history and literature. By integrating visual learning techniques, learners can deepen their understanding of this event and its broader historical context, while also exploring related literary works. Below is an example of how to implement a visual learning-focused lesson plan on the Boston Tea Party, incorporating multiple visual methods and providing adaptations for learners who need additional support.

Historical Study: The Boston Tea Party

1. Visual Timeline Creation:
- **Activity**: Begin by creating a visual timeline of the events leading up to the Boston Tea Party. Use a large poster or a digital timeline tool where learners can add images, drawings, and brief descriptions of key events, such as the Stamp Act, the Townshend Acts, and the Boston Massacre.
- **Visual Impact**: This timeline helps learners see the sequence of events and understand how tensions escalated between the American colonists and the British government, leading to the Boston Tea Party.

2. Reenacting the Boston Tea Party:
- **Activity:** Use role-playing to reenact the Boston Tea Party. Learners can create simple costumes, design props (like tea crates), and act out the event. This hands-on, visual approach makes the history come alive and helps learners internalize the significance of the protest.

- **Visual Storyboarding:** After the reenactment, have learners create a storyboard of the event, illustrating key moments from the protest and the reactions of both the colonists and the British.

3. Map Comparison Activity: Paul Revere's Ride:

- **Activity:** Provide learners with historical maps of Boston and the surrounding areas from the time of Paul Revere's famous ride. Compare these with modern maps to highlight how narrow and challenging the route was, particularly considering the limited access points to Boston due to rivers and British patrols.
- **Visual Exploration:** Learners can use markers or digital tools to trace Revere's route, noting key landmarks and obstacles. This visual exploration helps them appreciate the strategic importance of the ride and the geographical challenges Revere faced.
- Interactive Map Creation: Learners can also create their own simplified versions of the map, emphasizing the key points of Revere's journey, such as the Old North Church and the locations where he warned the militia. These maps can be displayed in the classroom as part of a larger visual exhibit on the event.

4. News Report: Write your own news story

- Activity: Conduct research online or at the local library on Paul Revere's Ride or a related event like the Battle of Lexington and Concord. Use only reputable sources such as vetted encyclopedias, historical organizations, and academic institutions.
- **Visual Exploration:** Learners can use story maps to break down the elements of a news story and then create their own. Using your notes and your map from activity three summarize the topic using a visual organization tool like the inverted paragraph (see figure below). Imagine you are a reporter during the colonial era and write your summary as a news brief of about 100 words.

* * *

136

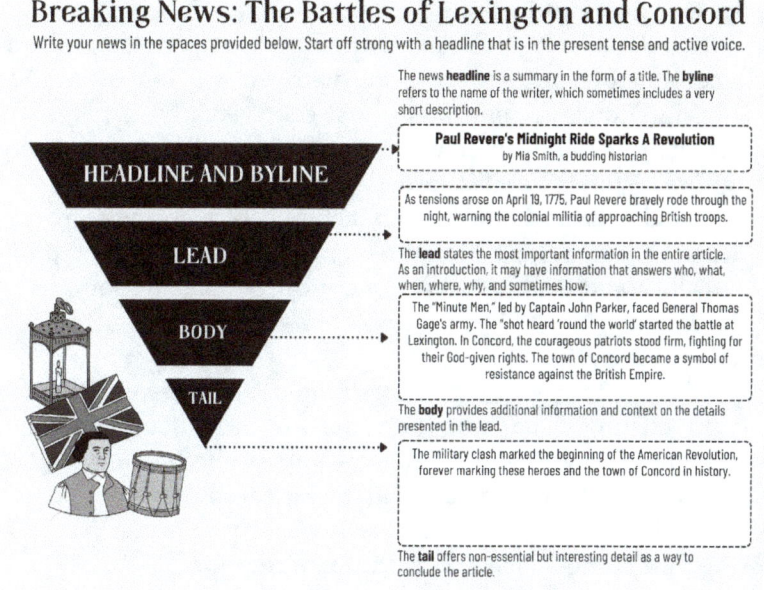

Breaking News: The Battles of Lexington and Concord

Write your news in the spaces provided below. Start off strong with a headline that is in the present tense and active voice.

The news **headline** is a summary in the form of a title. The **byline** refers to the name of the writer, which sometimes includes a very short description.

HEADLINE AND BYLINE

> **Paul Revere's Midnight Ride Sparks A Revolution**
> by Mia Smith, a budding historian

> As tensions arose on April 19, 1775, Paul Revere bravely rode through the night, warning the colonial militia of approaching British troops.

LEAD

The **lead** states the most important information in the entire article. As an introduction, it may have information that answers who, what, when, where, why, and sometimes how.

> The "Minute Men," led by Captain John Parker, faced General Thomas Gage's army. The "shot heard 'round the world" started the battle at Lexington. In Concord, the courageous patriots stood firm, fighting for their God-given rights. The town of Concord became a symbol of resistance against the British Empire.

BODY

The **body** provides additional information and context on the details presented in the lead.

TAIL

> The military clash marked the beginning of the American Revolution, forever marking these heroes and the town of Concord in history.

The **tail** offers non-essential but interesting detail as a way to conclude the article.

Literature Study: "Paul Revere's Ride" by Henry Wadsworth Longfellow

1. Visual Poem Analysis:

- **Activity:** Introduce learners to Henry Wadsworth Longfellow's poem "Paul Revere's Ride." As they read, provide a visual breakdown of the poem using a mind map. The mind map can illustrate the main themes, historical context, and key imagery in the poem.

- **Visual Reinforcement:** Have learners illustrate specific stanzas of the poem, either through drawing or by creating digital artwork. This helps them connect with the literary work on a deeper level and reinforces their understanding of the text.

- Create key concept or keyword cards that you illustrate to define words from the poem that learners may struggle with. More advanced learners can adapt the poem using modern language for a fun activity. Even asking a digital AI tool to take the poem and rewrite it in a modern style or to the tune of a favorite song can create an afternoon of fun.

137

* * *

2. Comparing Fact and Fiction:
- **Activity:** Create a Venn diagram to compare the historical account of Paul Revere's ride with the version presented in Longfellow's poem. Learners can visually organize the similarities and differences, noting where the poem diverges from historical facts for artistic or dramatic effect.
- **Visual Discussion:** Use this activity as a springboard for a discussion on how literature can shape our understanding of history, and the importance of critically analyzing sources.

3. Timeline Integration:
- **Activity:** Integrate the events from "Paul Revere's Ride" into the existing visual timeline of the Boston Tea Party. This shows learners how Revere's ride was part of the broader historical context, linking literature with historical study.

Adapting for Learners Needing Additional Support

For learners who need more support, particularly those with working memory challenges or attention difficulties, the following adaptations can be made:

- Simplified Visuals: Provide pre-made visual aids, such as simplified maps or partially completed storyboards, to reduce cognitive load. This allows learners to focus on key concepts without becoming overwhelmed by the details. Use stickers to annotate or digital tools to color in blocks for those working on small motor skills.
- **Guided Visual Tools:** Use guided mind maps or graphic organizers with prompts that help learners structure their thoughts. For example, a mind map for the poem might include branches labeled "Imagery," "Historical Context," and "Themes," with further prompts under each category.
- **Interactive Digital Tools:** Incorporate interactive digital tools that allow learners to engage with the material at their own pace. For example, use digital timelines or interactive maps that provide immediate feedback and allow learners to revisit information as needed.
- **Interactive Discussions:** Engage in interactive discussions

138

with your learner as you work through activities like creating the visual timeline or comparing maps. Ask open-ended questions to prompt critical thinking and encourage your learner to articulate their thoughts. For example, while comparing historical maps of Boston, ask, "What challenges do you think Paul Revere faced during his ride, given the narrow routes and British patrols?" You can have a multiple choice list that non-verbal learners can use to indicate their comprehension.

- **Co-Creating Visual Aids:** Work together with your learner to create visual aids such as storyboards, mind maps, or illustrations. For example, you can both take turns adding to a mind map of "Paul Revere's Ride" by Henry Wadsworth Longfellow, discussing the imagery and themes as you go. This collaborative effort allows you to guide your learner's understanding while actively involving them in the creative process.

- **Modeling Thought Processes:** As you work on activities, model your own thought processes aloud. For instance, while building the visual timeline of the Boston Tea Party, you might say, "I'm placing the Stamp Act here because it happened before the Boston Massacre. What do you think we should add next?" This helps your learner see how to organize and structure information visually.

- **Reflective Conversations:** After completing an activity, have a reflective conversation where you both discuss what was learned, what was challenging, and how the visual aids helped in understanding the material. This reinforces learning and helps your learner articulate their thoughts and insights.

By integrating visual learning techniques across both historical and literary studies, the story of the Boston Tea Party and Paul Revere's Ride becomes a rich, multifaceted learning experience. Learners not only gain a deeper understanding of these important historical events but also see how literature and history intersect, enriching their overall comprehension. These visual methods, combined with thoughtful adaptations for those needing additional support, create an inclusive and engaging educational environment that meets the diverse needs of all learners.

* * *

CONCLUSION

Visual reading strategies can make this fundamental skill more accessible and enjoyable for neurodivergent children. By understanding the neuroscience behind visual learning and implementing effective techniques, you can help your child build strong reading skills and a love for literature. This approach not only improves their comprehension but also fosters a lifelong passion for reading.

In the next chapter, we will explore how to support you, the guide, providing practical tips and techniques for building your confidence and your community as you embark on or expand your adventures in homeschooling!

PART THREE

SUPPORTING YOU, THE GUIDE

CHAPTER EIGHT

Confidence in Teaching

INTRODUCTION

Homeschooling a neurodivergent child is a journey filled with both rewards and challenges. As a parent-educator, your confidence and effectiveness are key to creating a supportive and enriching learning environment. It's also essential to recognize that it's okay to give yourself grace along the way. With days often filled with medical and therapy appointments, it can feel overwhelming to fit everything you want to accomplish into each day. But remember, homeschooling offers flexibility—learning doesn't have to be confined to the traditional hours of 9 to 3, Monday through Friday. Your homeschool structure can be as unique as your family. For instance, my family has found that schooling year-round works best for us, as it aligns with our schedule and helps prevent the regression that can occur during long breaks.

This chapter will explore general techniques for empowering yourself as an educator, delve into the neuroscience behind confidence and self-efficacy, and provide practical tips for building both your teaching skills and self-assurance. By embracing your unique approach and trusting in your ability to meet your child's needs, you can create a homeschooling experience that is both effective and fulfilling.

* * *

PERSONAL STORIES: A JOURNEY INTERRUPTED

Jamie, a bright and inquisitive autistic child with Down syndrome, had always been curious about the world. In elementary school, Jamie was part of an inclusion class, where they learned alongside their peers in a supportive environment. Jamie's teachers and parents worked together to nurture this curiosity, and despite the challenges of their diagnoses, Jamie showed a keen interest in a variety of subjects. Jamie loved asking questions—about how plants grew, why the stars twinkled, and what made cars move. Science experiments, storytime, and interactive learning activities captured Jamie's attention, and these moments of discovery filled Jamie's days with wonder.

However, as Jamie transitioned from elementary to middle school, everything changed. The school administration, citing Jamie's need for more specialized attention, decided to move Jamie from the academic path to a functional life skills classroom. This new environment was starkly different. The focus shifted away from academic subjects like science and history, and instead, Jamie spent much of the day learning how to sort silverware, fold laundry, and prepare simple meals. While these skills are important, they were presented in a way that limited Jamie, whose natural curiosity was now stifled by the lack of exposure to mathematics, science and the arts.

With each new school year, Jamie's enthusiasm for learning began to fade. The questions about the world that once bubbled out at every opportunity grew fewer and farther between. The classroom, which was supposed to help Jamie develop essential life skills, instead became a place where their intellectual growth seemed to stall. The vibrant discussions and hands-on experiments that once sparked Jamie's imagination were replaced with routines that felt disconnected from the interests that had once driven their love of learning. It wasn't that their supports were lacking or there was little care for Jaimie, just that the challenges focused more on daily skills and did not ignite curiosity in the why's of the world around them.

At the same time, Jamie's progress in social skills plateaued. In the inclusion classroom, Jamie had been surrounded by a diverse group of peers, which provided opportunities for social interaction and the development of communication skills. But in the functional life skills classroom, the social environment was more controlled and less varied, leading to fewer chances for meaningful interaction. Jaimie was mainly grouped with other peers that faced similar communication challenges and the diversity and resulting social challenges were lowered in complexity. As a result, Jamie stopped initiating conversations as frequently and withdrew into a quieter, more solitary space. The joy that had once come from sharing discoveries with others was replaced by a growing sense of isolation.

On reflection, Jamie's parents say they should have noticed these changes with more concern. They had always been Jamie's strongest advocates, and it pained them to realize how Jaimie's word choice had become so much more narrow. The child who had once eagerly explored the world around them was now more subdued, less engaged, and no longer as eager to ask the questions that had once driven their learning. Jamie's parents were so caught up in the day to day, they felt they didn't see the changes fast enough to understand what the outcome would be. They wished they would have pushed back on whether the functional life skills path was truly the best fit for their child. They understood that while the life skills being taught were valuable, they had not been enough to sustain Jamie's intellectual curiosity and social development.

Jamie's parents wished they had the chance to rewind time, and make a different decision at that pivotal moment when Jamie was moved from the academic path to the functional life skills classroom. Recognizing the spark of curiosity and love for learning that had always driven Jamie, they would have either insisted on classroom inclusion time or chosen to homeschool instead, creating a personalized learning environment that honored Jamie's intellectual interests at an appropriate level while still addressing the life skills needed for independence.

Even in a traditional classroom environment, Jaimie would have been exposed to literature and poetry. She could have participated by sequencing a story's plot line or participating in discussion groups. Jaimie could still have been exposed to those life skills by working together with another student as treasurer of a school club or as a wardrobe and props tech for the theatre department. Rather than limiting Jamie's education to sorting silverware and folding laundry, these practical tasks would be incorporated into a broader context that connected with Jamie's natural curiosity.

At home, Jaimie's parents started "extension schooling" as they didn't have the resources or schedule availability to homeschool. Extension schooling is doing an academic activity after school. It generally focuses on one topic at a time due to time constraints but allows for families to still customize their child's education. Jamie's parents tried looking for ways they could infuse history, science and math into Jaimie's daily tasks. For example, when teaching Jamie how to prepare simple meals, they integrated lessons about nutrition, food science, and the cultural significance of different dishes. Jamie learned not just how to make a sandwich, but also why certain foods are nutritious, how plants grow, and the science behind cooking techniques. This

146

approach turned every life skill into an opportunity for deeper exploration, making learning both functional and intellectually stimulating.

Science, which had always been Jamie's favorite subject as a younger learner, became a new focus after school. Jamie's parents introduced hands-on experiments that brought scientific concepts to life. Together, they built simple machines, grew plants from seeds, and observed the stars through a telescope. Jamie's questions about the world around them, which had once dwindled, were sparked back into life. With every experiment, Jamie's understanding of the natural world deepened, and the excitement of discovery reignited the curiosity that had been stifled in the functional classroom.

Jamie's parents also ensured that social interaction remained a key part of Jaimie's afterschool and weekend activities. They joined local a local adaptive sports team, where Jamie could interact with other children of varying ages and abilities. They also met up once a month for an adaptive nature class hosted by their city's parks department providing Jamie with additional social opportunities that had been lacking in the life skills classroom. Jamie began to initiate conversations again, sharing newfound knowledge with peers and building friendships based on common interests.

While not a full homeschool experience, the extension schooling focus allowed Jamie's parents to tailor some of the learning environment to Jamie's specific needs. They used visual aids, interactive learning tools, and Jamie's special interests—like superheroes—to make lessons more engaging. For instance, they created a series of lessons around each superhero's favorite style of transportation, exploring the history of flight, the science of locomotion, and even the math involved in planning car and train routes. This thematic approach not only made learning fun but also reinforced key academic skills through the lens of something Jamie loved.

As the months passed, Jamie's progress was remarkable. The plateau that had occurred in the life skills classroom was replaced by steady growth in both academic and social areas. Jamie's confidence blossomed as they mastered new concepts and skills, and the joy of learning returned in full force. The intentional dive into extension schooling, with its personalized approach and emphasis on curiosity-driven exploration, allowed Jamie to thrive in a way that expanded what she was learning in the traditional school setting.

This story of Jamie's journey reflects the importance of balancing functional skills with opportunities for academic growth and exploration, especially for children who thrive on curiosity and discovery. For Jamie, the shift away from an environment that nurtured these qualities led to a loss of enthusiasm for learning and social interaction, highlighting the need for educational approaches that honor both the practical and intellectual needs of every child. The decision to extension-school allowed Jamie's parents to provide an education that truly met their child's unique needs, fostering both the practical life skills necessary for independence and the academic curiosity that make learning a lifelong adventure.

* * *

GENERAL TECHNIQUES FOR BUILDING CONFIDENCE IN TEACHING

Confidence in teaching comes from a combination of knowledge, experience, and support. As you reflect on Jamie's story, it's clear that with the right approach, homeschooling can be a transformative experience for both you and your child. Whether you're fully homeschooling or incorporating extension schooling—supplementing your child's traditional education with additional learning opportunities at home—the following techniques can help you build your confidence and ensure that you are providing the best possible educational experience for your neurodivergent learner:

1. **Continuous Learning**: One of the most empowering steps you can take as a parent-educator is to stay informed about the latest research and best practices in education, especially for neurodivergent learners. Attend workshops, read relevant books, and participate in online courses that focus on homeschooling techniques, neurodiversity, and specialized learning strategies. Continuous learning not only enhances your teaching skills but also keeps you adaptable to your child's evolving needs. For example, understanding the neuroscience behind visual learning techniques can help you effectively implement them in subjects like math, science, and the humanities, making complex concepts more accessible to your learner.

2. **Embrace the Journey of Learning Together**: It's important to remember that you don't need to know everything when you start homeschooling, whether your learner is four years old or fifteen. Even after 17 years of homeschooling neurodivergent learners, I still don't always feel confident. Homeschooling is as much a journey for the parent as it is for the child. You are not expected to be an expert in every subject right away. Instead, embrace the process of learning alongside your child and allow yourself permission to make changes. This shared experience not only strengthens your bond but also models a growth mindset, showing your learner that it's okay to learn

new things at any age. Use resources, reach out to communities, and be open to discovering and mastering subjects together. The confidence to teach effectively will grow as you and your learner explore and learn side by side.

3. **Setting Realistic Goals and Managing Skill Development:** Confidence grows when you set and achieve goals, both for yourself and your child. Start by breaking down larger educational objectives into smaller, manageable steps that allow you to track progress and celebrate successes along the way. For example, a particularly effective tool for managing skill development is the use of picture schedules. Picture schedules are versatile and applicable for all ages, helping to maintain on-task behaviors and improve independence. You might start with hand-over-hand guidance, gradually transitioning to a picture schedule book. This book can list the tasks for the day, and as your learner becomes more independent, you can include the materials needed for each task. When your learner stalls or seems unsure of what to do next, you can gently guide them to refer to their book or schedule. Over time, you might shift from verbal cues to non-verbal prompts, encouraging them to independently consult their schedule. The key is to meet your learner where they are and guide them step by step towards greater independence. Remember, achieving the end goal takes time, and breaking it down into interim steps will prevent frustration for both you and your learner. [Spriggs[11]]

4. **Reflective Practice**: Regular reflection on your teaching methods and outcomes is a powerful tool for growth. Using smaller, more realistic goals provides you the opportunity to take time to identify what works well and what areas might need adjustment. For example, if you notice that your child responds particularly well to hands-on activities like building models or creating visual timelines, incorporate more of these strategies into your lessons. On the other hand, if a particular approach isn't resonating, don't hesitate to tweak it or try

---

[11] Spriggs, Amy D., et al. "Using Picture Activity Schedule Books to Increase On-Schedule and On-Task Behaviors." *Education and Training in Developmental Disabilities*, vol. 42, no. 2, 2007, pp. 209–23. *JSTOR*, http://www.jstor.org/stable/23879996. Accessed 6 Aug. 2024.

something new. Reflection allows you to be flexible and responsive, which is key to successful homeschooling.

5. **Seeking Support**: You don't have to navigate the homeschooling journey alone. Connecting with other homeschooling parents, educators, and support groups can provide invaluable insights, encouragement, and a sense of community. Whether you join local homeschooling co-ops, online forums, or attend homeschool conferences, these connections can offer fresh ideas, shared experiences, and moral support. Additionally, collaborating with others can introduce you to new resources and teaching techniques, such as integrating special interests into learning or using comics and visual models to explain complex concepts. If you are not sure what resources might be available to you, ask your local librarian. They will likely be able to point you to community groups, online support networks, and local resources that cater to both homeschoolers and the neurodivergent community.

6. **Self-Care and Balance**: To be an effective and confident educator, it's essential to prioritize your own well-being. Homeschooling, especially when managing additional responsibilities like medical appointments and therapy sessions, can be demanding. Ensure you maintain a healthy balance between teaching and personal time. This might mean scheduling regular breaks, setting aside time for your hobbies, or simply ensuring that you have quiet moments to recharge. Self-care is not just about physical health; it's also about mental and emotional well-being. By taking care of yourself, you'll be better equipped to handle the challenges of homeschooling and more confident in your role as an educator.

* * *

Exploring Extension Schooling

For parents who may not be ready to fully commit to homeschooling or who want to complement their child's traditional education, extension schooling offers a flexible alternative. This approach allows you to supplement your child's learning with additional activities and subjects that align with their interests and needs. For instance, if your child is passionate about a topic not covered in depth at school, such as astronomy or creative writing, you can create an extension curriculum that includes field trips, hands-on projects, and specialized resources.

Extension schooling also provides an opportunity to reinforce and expand on what your child is learning in their regular school setting. If your child struggles with a particular subject, you can use extension time to review and explore the material in different ways, such as through visual aids, experiments, or thematic units that tie together various aspects of their learning. This approach not only enhances your child's education but also builds your confidence in supporting their academic growth.

Moving Forward with Confidence

Homeschooling, whether full-time or as an extension of traditional schooling, is a journey that evolves with time and experience. By focusing on continuous learning, setting realistic goals, practicing reflection, seeking support, and prioritizing self-care, you can build the confidence needed to create a fulfilling and effective educational environment for your neurodivergent child. Remember, each step you take not only enhances your child's learning experience but also strengthens your own growth as a parent-educator. Embrace this journey with the understanding that your unique approach and dedication will make a lasting impact on your child's development and future.

THE NEUROSCIENCE BEHIND CONFIDENCE AND SELF-EFFICACY

Understanding the neuroscience behind confidence and self-efficacy can provide valuable insights into why certain techniques are effective, both for you as an educator and for your learner. Just as you work to build your child's confidence through carefully designed learning strategies, you can also harness these same principles to enhance your own teaching effectiveness and self-assurance.

Neuroplasticity: Building and Strengthening Neural Connections

The concept of neuroplasticity is foundational in understanding how both you and your learner can develop new skills and build confidence over time. Neuroplasticity refers to the brain's ability to reorganize itself by forming new neural connections, which means that with each new experience, your brain can adapt and grow. For educators, this means that every lesson you teach, every new technique you learn, and every challenge you overcome contributes to the development of your teaching skills.

Just as your learner's brain adapts when they practice new math problems or experiment with scientific concepts, your brain also strengthens connections as you gain experience in homeschooling. The more you engage in continuous learning—whether through workshops, books, or practical application—the more these neural pathways are reinforced. This process not only improves your teaching ability but also boosts your confidence, as you begin to see the positive effects of your efforts in your learner's progress. [Farrow12]

Positive Reinforcement: The Role of Dopamine in Confidence Building

Positive reinforcement plays a crucial role in building confidence and self-efficacy. When you experience success, your brain releases dopamine, a neurotransmitter associated with pleasure, reward, and motivation. This dopamine release reinforces the behavior that led to the success, making you more likely to repeat it in the future.

For example, when you successfully guide your learner through a challenging science experiment or help them understand a complex historical concept, the satisfaction you feel is not just emotional—it's chemical. This release of dopamine reinforces your confidence and motivates you to continue exploring and applying new teaching strategies. Celebrating small wins, both for yourself and your learner, is a powerful way to sustain this positive feedback loop. It's important to recognize that these moments of success, no matter how small, contribute significantly to building long-term confidence. [Friston13]

Stress Management: The Impact of Stress on Cognitive Function
* * *

---

12 Farrow, Tye. "The Study of Environmental Enrichment." *Constructing Health: How the Built Environment Enhances Your Mind's Health*, University of Toronto Press, 2024, pp. 77–83. *JSTOR*, http://www.jstor.org/stable/10.3138/jj.16394398.8. Accessed 13 Aug. 2024.

13 Friston, Karl, et al. "The Anatomy of Choice: Dopamine and Decision-Making." *Philosophical Transactions: Biological Sciences*, vol. 369, no. 1655, 2014, pp. 1–12. *JSTOR*, http://www.jstor.org/stable/24501930. Accessed 13 Aug. 2024.

While some stress can be motivating, high levels of chronic stress can impair cognitive function, making it harder to make decisions, think creatively, or solve problems. This is true for both educators and learners. When stress levels are high, the brain's ability to process information and respond effectively to challenges diminishes, which can negatively impact your confidence and teaching performance. [Öhman[14]]

Effective stress management techniques, such as mindfulness, relaxation exercises, and maintaining a healthy work-life balance, can mitigate these effects. By incorporating stress management into your routine, you can improve your cognitive function, enhance decision-making, and maintain a clear, focused mind. This not only makes you a more effective educator but also models healthy coping strategies for your learner, showing them how to manage their own stress in challenging situations.

Mirror Neurons: The Influence of Your Confidence on Your Learner

Mirror neurons are a fascinating aspect of neuroscience that highlights how your behavior and emotions can directly influence your learner. These neurons fire both when an individual performs an action and when they observe someone else performing that action. In the context of homeschooling, when your learner observes your confidence and calm demeanor, their mirror neurons can trigger similar feelings within them. This means that your confidence as an educator can positively impact your learner's own sense of self-efficacy. [Jeffers[15]]

For instance, if you approach a complex math problem with a calm and confident attitude, your learner is more likely to mirror that approach, feeling more confident in their own ability to tackle the problem. This reciprocal relationship between your confidence and your learner's confidence underscores the importance of maintaining a positive, assured approach to teaching.

---

[14] Öhman, Lena, et al. "Cognitive Function in Outpatients with Perceived Chronic Stress." *Scandinavian Journal of Work, Environment & Health*, vol. 33, no. 3, 2007, pp. 223–32. *JSTOR*, http://www.jstor.org/stable/40967646. Accessed 13 Aug. 2024.

[15] Jeffers, Carol S. "Within Connections: Empathy, Mirror Neurons, and Art Education." *Art Education*, vol. 62, no. 2, 2009, pp. 18–23. *JSTOR*, http://www.jstor.org/stable/27696326. Accessed 13 Aug. 2024.

* * *

The neuroscience behind confidence and self-efficacy reveals that both you and your learner have the potential to grow, adapt, and thrive through intentional practice and positive reinforcement. By understanding and applying these principles, you can enhance your own confidence as an educator, creating a more effective and supportive learning environment for your neurodivergent child. Just as you guide your learner through their educational journey, you are also on a journey of growth and development—one that is deeply influenced by the same neural processes that drive learning and confidence in your child. Embrace this journey with the knowledge that each step forward, no matter how small, is a significant stride towards becoming the confident, capable educator your child needs.

* * *

156

PRACTICAL TIPS FOR BUILDING CONFIDENCE IN TEACHING

Building confidence as a homeschool educator is a dynamic process that involves recognizing your strengths, staying flexible, celebrating progress, setting boundaries, and developing a strong support network. By integrating the elements discussed in previous sections, you can create a robust framework for growing your confidence and effectiveness in guiding your neurodivergent learner.

1. **Start with Strengths**: Begin by identifying your strengths as a teacher and use them as the cornerstone of your homeschooling approach. Perhaps you have a natural talent for storytelling, which you can leverage in teaching the humanities by using visual storytelling techniques, like creating comics or visual timelines. Or maybe you're particularly skilled in organizing and structuring lessons, which can be a great asset when designing math or science curricula that build on each concept incrementally. By recognizing and building on what you do well, you create a positive feedback loop that boosts your confidence and provides a solid foundation for further growth.

2. **Embrace Flexibility**: Flexibility is key to effective homeschooling, especially when working with neurodivergent learners. Be open to experimenting with different teaching methods and adapting your approach as needed. For example, if your child struggles with traditional approaches to math, try incorporating visual learning techniques like mind maps or interactive apps. If a particular science concept isn't clicking, consider a hands-on experiment or field trip to make it more tangible. Flexibility allows you to respond to your child's needs and preferences, leading to more effective and engaging learning experiences. Remember, what works today might need adjustment tomorrow, and that's okay—your willingness to adapt is a strength.

3. **Celebrate Progress**: Regularly acknowledging and celebrating both your child's progress and your achievements as a teacher is crucial for maintaining motivation and confidence. Positive reinforcement, as discussed in the neuroscience section,

releases dopamine, which boosts motivation and reinforces positive behaviors. Create rituals or routines around celebrating successes, whether it's finishing a challenging science project, mastering a new math concept, or completing a creative humanities assignment. These celebrations, no matter how small, help sustain the energy and enthusiasm needed to keep moving forward.

4. **Set Boundaries**: Establishing clear boundaries between teaching time and personal time is essential for preventing burnout and maintaining a healthy work-life balance. Just as you set specific goals and schedules for your learner, it's important to do the same for yourself. Designate specific times for teaching, planning, and personal activities, and be disciplined about sticking to these boundaries. This helps ensure that you have the energy and focus needed to be an effective educator while also taking care of your own well-being. Remember, taking time for yourself is not a luxury—it's a necessity that enables you to bring your best self to your child's education.

5. **Develop a Support Network**: Building a strong support network is one of the most effective ways to boost your confidence as a homeschool educator. Connect with other homeschooling parents, educators, and professionals who can offer advice, share resources, and provide moral support. This network can be invaluable when you face challenges, whether it's finding the right approach to a difficult subject or simply needing encouragement on a tough day. Join local homeschooling groups, participate in online forums, and attend workshops or conferences to expand your network. Feeling connected and supported not only enhances your confidence but also enriches your homeschooling experience by exposing you to new ideas and perspectives. Remind yourself that you are not the only one homeschooling a neurodivergent child. Don't be afraid to join general homeschooling groups with the fear that your child will be the odd one out. You and your child are members of the same community as they are and providing the community at large with opportunities to demonstrate inclusion may delightfully surprise you.

6. **Leverage Visual Learning Techniques**: As you develop your

homeschooling approach, consider integrating visual learning techniques across all subjects. For example, use picture schedules to help your learner stay on task and build independence, or create visual models to explain complex science concepts. In the humanities, consider using graphic novels or visual timelines to make historical events more relatable. These techniques, which have been discussed throughout this guide, are powerful tools for making learning more accessible and engaging for neurodivergent learners. By becoming proficient in these methods, you'll enhance your teaching skills and increase your confidence in delivering effective instruction.

7. **Engage in Reflective Practice**: Regular reflection on your teaching methods and outcomes allows you to continuously improve your approach. Take time at the end of each week to review what worked well and what didn't, and make adjustments as needed. This reflective practice helps you stay attuned to your learner's evolving needs and ensures that you're always moving toward more effective teaching strategies. Additionally, reflection provides an opportunity to acknowledge your own growth as an educator, reinforcing your confidence and commitment to the homeschooling journey.

* * *

Finding Community is Essential

Moving Forward with Confidence

By starting with your strengths, staying flexible, celebrating progress, setting clear boundaries, developing a support network, leveraging visual learning techniques, and engaging in reflective practice, you can build the confidence needed to excel as a homeschool educator. These practical tips, rooted in the experiences and neuroscience principles discussed earlier, provide a comprehensive approach to growing your skills and self-assurance. As you continue on this journey, remember that confidence is built over time, through experience, reflection, and the support of a community that shares your commitment to providing the best possible education for your neurodivergent learner.

* * *

PRACTICAL TIPS FOR CONTINUOUS IMPROVEMENT

Continuous improvement as a homeschool educator is essential to adapting and growing alongside your learner. By staying informed, experimenting with new methods, seeking feedback, reflecting on your experiences, and maintaining a positive mindset, you can create a dynamic and responsive learning environment that meets your child's evolving needs.

1. **Stay Informed**: Knowledge is power, and staying informed is key to continuous improvement. Regularly update your understanding of homeschooling practices, neurodivergent education, and effective teaching strategies by reading books, attending webinars, and joining online communities. These resources provide fresh perspectives, innovative ideas, and the latest research, all of which can enhance your approach to teaching. For example, learning about the latest neuroscience behind visual learning can introduce new ways to make abstract concepts more accessible for your learner.

2. **Experiment with Methods**: Don't be afraid to experiment with different teaching methods and tools. Every learner is unique, and what works for one child might not work for another. By being open to trying new approaches, you may discover highly effective strategies that resonate with your child's learning style. For instance, if traditional text-based learning doesn't seem to be working, consider incorporating more hands-on activities, visual aids, or thematic units that align with your child's interests. I learned, for example, through experimentation that my own learner does well at processing audiobooks so we pull one up while driving places and can get through several chapters throughout the week's therapy runs. Experimentation allows you to tailor your teaching methods to your learner's needs, ensuring a more personalized and effective education.

3. **Seek Feedback**: Feedback is a powerful tool for growth. Regularly seek verbal and non-verbal feedback from your child, observing their reactions and responses to different teaching methods, and from other educators or homeschooling parents. Constructive feedback can provide valuable insights

that help you fine-tune your approach. Remember, feedback isn't just about identifying areas for improvement; it's also about recognizing what's working well and building on those successes. By incorporating feedback into your practice, you can continuously refine your teaching strategies to better support your learner.

4. **Reflect and Adjust**: Reflection is a critical component of continuous improvement. Take time to regularly reflect on your teaching experiences, assessing what worked, what didn't, and why. This reflection helps you identify patterns and trends in your learner's progress, allowing you to make informed adjustments to your approach. For example, if you notice that your child engages more with visual storytelling than with traditional lectures, you can incorporate more visual elements into your lessons. Reflecting on your experiences not only enhances your teaching effectiveness but also reinforces your confidence as an educator.

5. **Presume Competence**: One of the most important principles in homeschooling, especially for neurodivergent learners, is to always presume competence. This means believing in your learner's ability to understand and process information, even when it's not immediately apparent. Teaching a low-verbal learner can sometimes make it challenging to gauge how much is being absorbed and generalized, but it's crucial to trust in their potential. I had a personal experience with this while teaching my child about Viking history and religion. I tried multiple visual models, videos, graphic novels, and games, but it felt like the concepts weren't sinking in. I was discouraged, unsure of how much my child was learning. It felt like I had been talking to myself for nearly the entire topic. Then, a few weeks later, while on a hike, we came across a sign warning against swimming near a waterfall due to the dangerous undertow. The sign documented the number of drowning deaths that had occurred at that spot. Out of the blue, my child said, "I guess they are with Rán now," referring to the Norse goddess of the sea who collects lost souls that drown. In that moment, I realized that not only had my child been listening, but they had also understood and had generalized the information. I was dumbfounded, relieved, reinvigorated and ecstatic all at the same time. This experience reinforced the

162

importance of presuming competence and trusting in the learning process, even when progress isn't immediately visible.

Rán, the Norse goddess of the sea

6. **Maintain a Positive Mindset**: A positive mindset is essential for resilience and continuous improvement. Homeschooling can be challenging, and it's easy to become discouraged when things don't go as planned. However, focusing on the positive aspects of your teaching journey can help you navigate challenges more effectively. Celebrate small victories, both yours and your learner's, and view setbacks as opportunities for growth rather than failures. A positive mindset not only enhances your own resilience but also models a constructive approach to challenges for your learner, teaching them the

value of perseverance and optimism.

Moving Forward with Continuous Improvement

Continuous improvement is not a destination but a journey—one that evolves as you and your learner grow together. By staying informed, experimenting with new methods, seeking feedback, reflecting on your experiences, presuming competence in your learner, and maintaining a positive mindset, you can create a dynamic and effective homeschooling environment. These practices not only enhance your teaching abilities but also ensure that your child receives a tailored education that meets their unique needs. Remember, every step you take toward improving your teaching practice is a step toward a richer, more fulfilling learning experience for your child.

CONCLUSION

Building confidence as a homeschool educator is a journey that requires continuous learning, reflection, and support. This chapter has explored how understanding the neuroscience behind confidence and self-efficacy can empower you to become a more effective and assured teacher. By integrating practical strategies such as starting with your strengths, embracing flexibility, celebrating progress, and setting boundaries, you lay the foundation for a positive and dynamic learning environment.

We've also discussed the importance of presuming competence in your learner, recognizing that, even when it's challenging to gauge their understanding, they are often absorbing and processing information in ways that may surprise you. The story of how my child unexpectedly demonstrated their understanding of Viking history reminds us of the profound impact that patience, trust, and tailored learning approaches can have on our children's educational journey.

Moreover, we've highlighted the value of continuous improvement through regular reflection, experimentation, and seeking feedback. These practices not only enhance your teaching skills but also ensure that your homeschool curriculum evolves to meet your child's unique needs. By staying informed and connected with a support network, you can draw strength and inspiration from others on similar paths, further boosting your confidence and effectiveness as an educator.

As you move forward, remember that homeschooling is as much about your growth as it is about your child's. Each new technique you try, every small victory you celebrate, and each adjustment you make contributes to a more enriching educational experience for both you and your learner. This journey may be challenging at times, but with the right mindset and support, it is incredibly rewarding.

In the next chapter, we will delve into the importance of finding community and resources. We will provide practical tips for connecting with other homeschooling families, accessing valuable support, and gathering the information you need to continue growing in your role as an educator. By building a strong community around you, you will find that the journey of homeschooling becomes not only manageable but also deeply fulfilling, both for you and your neurodivergent child.

* * *

CRAFTING

BIKING

SWIMMING

NATURE WALK

BUILDING BLOCKS

SCIENCE EXPERIMENT

OUTDOOR PLAY UP

PLAYGROUND

KITE FLYING

Visual Schedules Encourage Independence

CHAPTER NINE

Community and Resources

INTRODUCTION

One of the most important aspects of homeschooling, especially when teaching a neurodivergent child, is having access to a supportive community and valuable resources. These elements can provide essential guidance, encouragement, and practical tools to enhance your homeschooling journey. This chapter explores the importance of community, identifies key resources, and offers practical tips for connecting with other homeschooling families and accessing support.

PERSONAL STORIES: BUILDING A SUPPORTIVE COMMUNITY

Jessica, a mother of a neurodivergent teenager named Ethan, began her homeschooling journey with a mix of determination and trepidation. She knew that traditional school settings weren't meeting Ethan's needs, but the idea of taking on his education herself was daunting. The early days of homeschooling were challenging—Jessica often felt overwhelmed by the responsibility and isolated in her efforts to provide the best learning environment for her son. Without a clear roadmap or support system, she found herself struggling to navigate the complexities of educating a neurodivergent learner on her own.

* * *

Desperate for guidance and connection, Jessica decided to search for others who might be experiencing the same challenges. She joined an online forum specifically for parents of neurodivergent children who were homeschooling. This decision marked a turning point in her journey. Through the online community, Jessica found not only practical advice and resources but also the emotional support she had been lacking. Parents from all over the country shared their successes and struggles, offering tips on everything from curriculum choices to managing daily routines. Jessica no longer felt alone—she realized that there were many other parents out there facing similar challenges and that together, they could learn and grow.

Buoyed by the support she found online, Jessica decided to take the next step and seek out local connections. She discovered a homeschooling conference in her area and decided to attend, even though the idea of meeting new people was outside her comfort zone. The conference proved to be an eye-opening experience. Jessica connected with other parents who shared her concerns and aspirations for their children. She attended workshops on homeschooling techniques for neurodivergent learners, participated in discussions about educational strategies, and found herself inspired by the stories of other homeschooling families.

The connections Jessica made at the conference were invaluable. She realized that, while the online community provided a great deal of support, there was something uniquely powerful about face-to-face interactions. She left the conference feeling energized and motivated to build a local network of support. Drawing on the inspiration and knowledge she had gained, Jessica took the bold step of starting a local support group for homeschooling parents of neurodivergent children.

The group began with just a few families meeting informally at a local park, but it quickly grew as word spread. Jessica organized regular meetups where parents could share resources, discuss challenges, and simply enjoy each other's company. These gatherings became a lifeline for many parents, offering a safe space to vent, laugh, and learn together. The group also provided much-needed socialization opportunities for the children, who formed friendships and engaged in collaborative learning activities that complemented their individual homeschooling efforts.

For Jessica and Ethan, this community became a cornerstone of their homeschooling experience. Ethan, who had once struggled with feelings of isolation, began to thrive socially and academically. He enjoyed participating in the group's projects and outings, and Jessica noticed a marked improvement in his confidence and engagement with learning. For Jessica, the group offered a sense of belonging and reassurance that she was on the right path. She no longer felt like she was homeschooling in a vacuum—she had a community of parents who understood her journey and were there to support her every step of the way.

Looking back, Jessica realized that finding and building a supportive community had transformed not only her approach to homeschooling but also her relationship with her son. The connections she made—

both online and in person—provided her with the tools, encouragement, and friendship she needed to succeed as a homeschool educator. Jessica's journey is a testament to the power of community in turning what once felt like an overwhelming challenge into a rewarding and fulfilling experience for both her and Ethan.

THE IMPORTANCE OF COMMUNITY IN HOMESCHOOLING

Community is a vital component of a successful homeschooling journey, providing numerous benefits that extend beyond academic support. For homeschooling families, particularly those with neurodivergent learners, a strong community can be a source of emotional, intellectual, and social enrichment. Engaging with your community independently or with organized groups can profoundly impact both you and your learner:

- **Emotional Support:** Homeschooling, while rewarding, can sometimes feel isolating, especially when you're navigating the unique challenges of teaching a neurodivergent child. Connecting with other homeschooling parents who share similar experiences offers emotional support, helping you feel less isolated and more understood. The reassurance that comes from sharing experiences, challenges, and successes with others who truly "get it" can be invaluable. This emotional connection not only alleviates stress but also fosters a sense of belonging and shared purpose.
- **Sharing Resources and Ideas:** One of the most practical benefits of community involvement is the exchange of resources, ideas, and teaching strategies. By participating in a homeschool community, you can tap into a wealth of collective knowledge and experience. Whether it's discovering new visual learning tools, experimenting with innovative teaching methods, or finding the best local resources for your child's specific needs, the community can be an endless source of inspiration. This collaborative approach enhances your ability to adapt and refine your homeschooling practices, leading to continuous improvement in your teaching.
- **Social Skill Development Opportunities**: Social skills are

often a concern for neurodivergent homeschooling families, but being part of a group and getting out in the community addresses this need effectively. For children, community interactions provide valuable opportunities to make friends, engage in group activities, and develop social skills in a supportive environment. For neurodivergent learners, these social interactions can be particularly beneficial, offering them a safe space to practice communication and social cues in a variety of contexts. Moreover, as a parent, building meaningful connections with other homeschooling parents provides you with a network of peers who understand your journey, offering camaraderie and support.

- **Collaborative Learning**: Homeschooling communities often organize collaborative learning experiences, such as field trips, co-op classes, and group projects. These activities enrich the homeschooling experience by providing diverse learning opportunities that might not be available at home. Collaborative learning not only introduces your child to different perspectives and teaching styles but also enhances their ability to work with others, fostering teamwork and communication skills. Additionally, these shared educational experiences can make learning more engaging and memorable, reinforcing the concepts and skills being taught.

- **Neurological Benefits of Community Engagement**: Engaging with a community offers neurological benefits that are essential for both you and your learner. Social interaction and emotional support from a community can reduce stress and improve cognitive function by increasing the release of neurotransmitters like dopamine and oxytocin, which are associated with pleasure, reward, and social bonding. [ref[16]] For your learner, participating in community activities can help reinforce their learning through repetition and social reinforcement, aiding in the retention and generalization of knowledge. For you, being part of a supportive community can enhance your confidence and self-efficacy as an educator, as the positive experiences and feedback you receive help

---

[16] Ochs, Elinor, and Olga Solomon. "Autistic Sociality." *Ethos*, vol. 38, no. 1, 2010, pp. 69–92. *JSTOR*, http://www.jstor.org/stable/40603401. Accessed 6 Aug. 2024.

strengthen the neural pathways associated with learning and growth.

Incorporating community into your homeschooling journey is not just about socializing or sharing resources—it's about creating a network of support that nurtures both your child's development and your growth as an educator. The emotional, intellectual, and neurological benefits of community engagement make it a powerful tool for enriching the homeschooling experience. By actively participating in a supportive community, you are investing in the well-being and success of your family's educational journey, ensuring that both you and your learner have the support and resources needed to thrive.

* * *

172

IDENTIFYING KEY RESOURCES

Building a strong community is essential for a successful homeschooling journey, especially when teaching neurodivergent children. Connecting with others not only provides emotional and educational support but also opens up a wealth of resources that can enhance your homeschooling experience. Here's how you can identify key resources and effectively connect with the homeschooling community:

1. **Join Online Communities**: Online communities and forums are a great starting point for connecting with other homeschooling parents, especially those focused on neurodivergent learners. Platforms like Facebook, Meetup, Reddit, and specialized homeschooling websites offer spaces where you can participate in discussions, ask questions, and share experiences. These communities are invaluable for exchanging ideas, discovering new teaching strategies, and finding support from others who understand your journey.

2. **Leverage Your Local Library and Community Centers**: Your local library is a versatile resource that can help you connect with other homeschooling families and find educational materials. Many libraries offer programs, workshops, and events specifically for homeschoolers, and librarians can often provide information on local homeschooling groups and educational resources. Additionally, community centers and learning centers frequently host classes, tutoring sessions, and extracurricular activities that can enrich your homeschooling curriculum.

3. **Attend Local Events and Meetups**: Actively seek out local homeschooling events, such as meetups, workshops, and conferences. These gatherings provide opportunities to connect with other homeschooling families, share experiences, and learn from one another. If you're looking for a community that aligns with your specific needs, such as those focused on neurodivergence, these events can be particularly valuable in finding like-minded families and resources that suit your child's learning style.

4. **Explore Local and Specialized Organizations**: There are

numerous organizations dedicated to supporting neurodivergent learners and their families. Groups like Labeled and Loved, which offers Virtual Sisterhood Circles (labeledandloved.org), provide online support systems where moms can connect for a supportive hour with other moms that "get it". These organizations often offer tailored advice, advocacy, and materials that can be incredibly beneficial in shaping your homeschooling approach. Other organizations like the Autism Society, CHADD (Children and Adults with Attention-Deficit/Hyperactivity Disorder), and Understood.org offer tailored advice, educational materials, and tools to help you navigate the homeschooling journey. Additionally, ask for recommendations at your child's therapy or medical appointments—they may be aware of local resources, support groups, or specialized programs that can enhance your homeschooling experience.

5. **Use Social Media for Local and Virtual Connections**: Social media platforms are powerful tools for finding both local and virtual homeschooling communities. Many homeschooling groups have dedicated pages or groups on platforms like Facebook, where members can share resources, organize meetups, and provide support to one another. These connections can be particularly helpful for staying informed about local events, finding nearby families with similar homeschooling goals, and accessing a broader range of educational resources.

6. **Start or Join a Homeschool Group**: If you discover that there isn't an existing homeschool group in your area that meets your needs, consider starting one. Organize regular meetings, field trips, and collaborative learning activities that align with the interests and needs of your child and others in the community. By taking the initiative to create a group, you can foster a supportive network that benefits all involved.

7. **Volunteer and Participate in Community Activities**: Engaging in community activities and volunteering your time and skills can help you build connections and contribute to the homeschooling community. Whether it's organizing a local event, leading a workshop, or participating in community service projects, active involvement helps you connect with others and build a strong support network. Providing

volunteer opportunities for your learner can also prepare them with valuable social and job skills. Think about visiting a food pantry to help fill up weekly boxes in the warehouse or volunteering at the library to help reshelve books.

8. **Connecting in Rural Areas**: For families living in rural areas, where access to groups and meetups may be limited, creativity and resourcefulness are key. Local businesses can be excellent partners in your homeschooling journey—consider asking a local café, grocery store, or farm if they would be willing to host a demonstration or provide a tour. These experiences not only offer practical learning opportunities but also allow your child to practice social skills in real-world settings. You can use everyday activities like ordering food at a café or selecting ingredients for a recipe at the grocery store to reinforce social interaction and independence. Additionally, consider forming a small cooperative with nearby families to rotate hosting educational activities, or use virtual platforms to connect with other rural homeschooling families. Another idea is to take advantage of outdoor learning opportunities—nature walks, visits to local parks, or even gardening can provide rich, hands-on learning experiences that foster curiosity and engagement. Lastly, don't underestimate the value of local community members; retired professionals, artisans, or hobbyists in your area may be willing to share their knowledge and skills with your child, offering unique learning opportunities that are both personal and impactful.

* * *

Connecting with a supportive community and identifying key resources are crucial steps in creating a successful homeschooling experience for your neurodivergent child. Whether you're in an urban area with many resources or a rural area with fewer options, there are creative ways to build a network that provides the support, ideas, and encouragement you need. By joining online communities, attending local events, leveraging your library and community resources, and using social media, you can create a rich and supportive educational environment. Remember, you are not alone on this journey—there are countless resources and communities ready to help you and your child thrive.

CONCLUSION

* * *

Building a supportive community and accessing valuable resources are not just helpful—they are essential to a successful and fulfilling homeschooling journey, particularly when educating a neurodivergent child. Throughout this chapter, we've explored the profound impact that community can have on both you and your learner, from providing emotional support and sharing resources to offering opportunities for socialization and collaborative learning. Whether you are engaging with online forums, leveraging local libraries, attending homeschooling conferences, or forming small groups in rural areas, these connections enrich your experience and create a network of support that is invaluable.

We've also discussed the importance of continuously identifying and utilizing key resources, including educational websites, local homeschool groups, and specialized organizations that cater to the needs of neurodivergent learners. These resources, combined with the collective knowledge and encouragement found within a community, empower you as an educator and enhance your child's learning environment.

For those in rural areas, we've highlighted the creative ways you can build a community and create rich learning experiences, even when traditional resources may be scarce. From partnering with local businesses for educational tours to practicing social skills in everyday settings, these strategies ensure that your child receives a well-rounded education, regardless of location.

Furthermore, we've touched on the neurological benefits of community engagement, such as reducing stress and enhancing cognitive function, which play a critical role in both your effectiveness as an educator and your child's development. The story of Jessica and her son Ethan illustrates the transformative power of finding and building a supportive community. Their journey from isolation to thriving within a network of like-minded families serves as a powerful reminder that you are not alone in this endeavor.

As you move forward, remember that the connections you build, the resources you utilize, and the communities you engage with all contribute to creating a more effective and supportive learning environment for your neurodivergent child. These elements are the foundation of a successful homeschooling journey, providing both you and your child with the tools, encouragement, and companionship needed to thrive.

In the next chapter, we will explore how to continuously adapt and grow as an educator. We'll provide practical tips for ongoing improvement, ensuring that you and your child continue to flourish in your homeschooling journey. By embracing the principles of lifelong learning and continuous adaptation, you can ensure that your educational approach remains dynamic, responsive, and deeply enriching for your learner.

CHAPTER TEN

Your Homeschool Journey

INTRODUCTION

Embarking on the homeschooling journey with a neurodivergent child can be daunting, filled with uncertainties and challenges. However, with dedication, adaptability, and the right strategies, it is possible to create a supportive and enriching learning environment that fosters your child's growth and development. This final chapter reflects on the overall homeschooling journey, offering encouragement, practical advice, and final thoughts to help you transition from uncertainty to confidence.

PERSONAL STORIES: FINDING THE RIGHT FIT

Emily's Journey to Effective Blended Micro-Schooling and Homeschooling

Kari, a mother committed to providing the best education for her neurodivergent daughter, Emily, faced a critical decision as Emily was entering high school. Emily had always struggled in the traditional school environment—not only was she not thriving academically, but she also faced severe bullying and social pressures. Emily, who was exploring her identity on the gender and sexuality spectrum, found the school environment increasingly hostile. The constant bullying was taking a toll on her spirit, leaving her feeling unsafe and unsupported. The stress and anxiety from these experiences made it impossible for Emily to focus on her studies, and Kari knew that something had to change.

After much consideration, Kari and her husband, Mark, decided to pull Emily out of the traditional school system. They enrolled her in a micro-school specifically designed to be a safe haven for neurodivergent learners. This micro-school was different—it followed a democratic education model, where students managed their own learning and participated in the governance of the school. Daily meetings were held where every student, including Emily, had a vote and could bring up new agenda items for the group to consider. This democratic approach fostered a sense of ownership and empowerment among the students, creating a community where Emily finally felt safe, respected, and valued.

The micro-school's inclusive and supportive environment was exactly what Emily needed. She was surrounded by other neurodivergent learners who understood her challenges and accepted her for who she was. The school's focus on creating a welcoming and safe space allowed Emily to explore her identity without fear of judgment or ridicule. With the pressures of traditional school behind her, Emily began to engage more fully in her education, particularly in subjects like science, where she could participate in group experiments and hands-on learning activities.

Micro-schools are usually set up so that they students attend 2-3 days a week with the other days to be used for personal projects and self-study. Kari and Mark, who both worked remotely, decided to blend Emily's micro-schooling with part-time homeschooling. This approach allowed them to be actively involved in Emily's education while also giving her the social interaction and collaborative learning experiences she thrived on at the micro-school. At home, Kari focused on project-based learning, a method that had always resonated with Emily. They embarked on creative projects that tied into Emily's interests, such as running virtual ecology models to explore animal biology and ecosystems. Kari used interactive digital tools to complement these projects, offering Emily a dynamic and personalized learning experience.

This blended approach allowed Emily to experience the best of both worlds. At her micro-school, she enjoyed the camaraderie of her peers and the freedom to direct her own learning within a supportive, democratic community. At home, Kari's project-based learning approach provided a more personalized, interest-driven education that aligned with Emily's specific needs and passions. The combination of these two settings created a rich and varied educational experience that kept Emily engaged, challenged, and excited about learning.

Kari and Mark's journey wasn't without its challenges. Balancing work, homeschooling, and ensuring that Emily's time at the micro-school was productive required careful planning and continuous adaptation. Kari made it a priority to regularly reflect on their approach, discussing with Mark what was working and where adjustments might be needed. They also sought feedback from Emily, paying close attention to her reactions and preferences. If Emily seemed particularly interested in a topic she encountered at the micro-school, Kari would extend that learning at home with related projects or further exploration. Conversely, if a homeschooling method didn't resonate with Emily, Kari was quick to pivot, trying new strategies until they found what worked best.

Through this ongoing process of reflection, experimentation, and adaptation, Kari and Mark developed a homeschooling approach that was as dynamic and evolving as Emily herself. They realized that their approach to educating Emily didn't have to fit into a single mold—it could be a blend of several different methods, each tailored to Emily's needs at any given time. Whether it was project-based learning at home or hands-on science experiments at her micro-school, every aspect of Emily's education was thoughtfully integrated to provide a cohesive, engaging learning experience.

Kari's dedication to continuous improvement in Emily's education not only led to significant academic progress but also strengthened their family bond. Emily's confidence grew as she saw herself succeeding in both her micro-school and home projects, and Kari felt a deep sense of fulfillment in knowing that they had created an educational environment where Emily could truly thrive.

* * *

Kari's story illustrates that successful homeschooling doesn't have to be an all-or-nothing endeavor. By blending different approaches—micro-schooling for social interaction and hands-on learning, and homeschooling for personalized, interest-driven education—Kari and Mark were able to craft an educational experience that was uniquely suited to Emily. Their journey highlights the importance of flexibility, continuous reflection, and the willingness to adapt, ensuring that Emily's education remains as dynamic and multifaceted as her interests and needs.

REFLECTING ON THE JOURNEY

The homeschooling journey is unique for every family, marked by both successes and challenges. As the primary guide in your child's education, taking time to reflect on your experiences is crucial for appreciating the progress you've made and understanding the lessons learned along the way. This reflection not only helps you celebrate accomplishments but also provides valuable insights into how to continuously adapt and improve your approach.

Celebrate Milestones

Homeschooling offers the opportunity to create a deeply personalized education, where each milestone, no matter how small, is significant. Take time to celebrate the achievements in subjects like math, science, and the humanities. Whether your learner has mastered a challenging concept in math, constructed a detailed science model, or completed a creative humanities project, these moments of success deserve recognition. Celebrating these milestones reinforces the positive aspects of your journey and boosts your child's confidence. It also serves as a reminder of the progress you both have made, particularly in areas where your child may have struggled initially.

For example, if your learner was once intimidated by abstract math concepts but has now successfully factored a complex polynomial using visual aids, this is a major milestone. Find a template for an award certificate and create a special place in your home where you celebrate your learner's achievements! Seeing that wall will show your learner that what they did was important and they will gain an enormous sense of pride. Similarly, completing a hands-on science experiment, like constructing a DNA model or exploring cell mitosis through a comic strip, is an accomplishment worth celebrating. In the humanities, maybe your learner crafted a compelling visual story about a historical event or analyzed literature in a way that resonated with them personally. These achievements are the building blocks of their education and should be acknowledged with pride.

Acknowledge Challenges

Homeschooling is a journey filled with challenges, and reflecting on these difficulties is essential for growth. Consider the obstacles you've faced—whether it's finding the right resources, adapting to your child's unique learning style, or balancing multiple subjects—and how you've overcome them. Acknowledging these challenges is not about focusing on the negative, but rather about recognizing your resilience and the strategies you've developed along the way.

For instance, if you encountered difficulties in keeping your learner engaged with traditional reading methods, you might have adapted by incorporating visual learning strategies such as comics or graphic novels. Reflect on how these adaptations have not only addressed the challenges but also enriched your learner's experience. Perhaps in science, you struggled to explain abstract concepts, leading you to create more hands-on experiments and models. Acknowledging how these challenges were turned into opportunities for creative solutions provides valuable insights for future learning experiences. Journaling about your struggles and what solutions you discovered along the way can provide some needed motivation on those low days.

Appreciate Growth

Homeschooling is a transformative journey that extends far beyond academics. Reflect on the personal growth and development that both you and your child have experienced. Consider how your child's understanding of subjects like math, science, and the humanities has deepened, but also how their confidence, curiosity, and love for learning have flourished.

For example, if your learner began with a limited understanding of historical events and now actively engages in creating visual timelines and storyboards, this growth is worth appreciating. Similarly, their progression from struggling with scientific concepts to confidently conducting experiments and building models reflects not just academic achievement, but also personal development in problem-solving and critical thinking.

As a guide, your growth is equally important. Reflect on how you've adapted your teaching strategies, learned to be more patient and creative, and become more attuned to your child's needs and strengths. Homeschooling challenges you to grow alongside your learner, and recognizing this mutual development can be incredibly rewarding.

Moving Forward

As you reflect on your homeschooling journey, use these insights to continue evolving your approach. Celebrate the milestones, learn from the challenges, and appreciate the growth that has occurred. This reflection will not only enhance your homeschooling experience but also strengthen the bond between you and your child, as you both continue to learn and grow together.

PRACTICAL ADVICE FOR ONGOING SUCCESS

As you navigate your homeschooling journey, especially with a neurodivergent learner, it's important to remember that success comes from a combination of realistic expectations, a positive environment, open communication, and ongoing personal growth. Here's a blended guide that incorporates practical advice with key points of encouragement and support to help you continue thriving as an educator and parent.

1. **Set Realistic Expectations**: Focus on setting achievable goals for both yourself and your child. Avoid the temptation to compare your homeschooling journey with others, as each family's experience is unique. What works best for your child may be different from what works for others. Establish milestones that reflect your child's individual progress and celebrate those achievements.
2. **Create a Positive Learning Environment:** Foster a learning

environment that is both positive and nurturing, where curiosity and exploration are encouraged. Tailor the learning experience to your child's interests, making it enjoyable and relevant. Whether it's through project-based learning, hands-on experiments, or creative arts, ensure that your child feels engaged and excited about their education.

3. **Maintain Open Communication:** Keep the lines of communication open with your child. Regularly discuss their learning experiences, interests, and any challenges they may face. This dialogue not only strengthens your relationship but also helps you adapt your teaching methods to better suit their needs. Encourage your child to express their thoughts and feelings, and be responsive to their feedback.

4. **Prioritize Self-Care**: A balanced lifestyle is crucial for both you and your child. Ensure that your homeschooling schedule includes time for relaxation, physical activity, and downtime. Taking care of your mental and physical health allows you to bring your best self to your role as an educator. Remember, self-care is not just about rest—it's about nurturing your well-being so that you can continue to support your child's growth effectively.

5. **Continue Learning and Growing**: Stay committed to continuous improvement in your homeschooling practice. Regularly update your knowledge, experiment with new teaching methods, and be open to feedback and adaptation. Homeschooling is an evolving journey, and your willingness to learn and grow alongside your child will enhance the educational experience for both of you.

6. **Trust Yourself**: Trust in your ability to educate and support your child. You know your child best, and your dedication and love are powerful tools in their education. It's natural to have moments of doubt, but remember that your commitment to your child's well-being and education is what matters most.

7. **Seek Support:** Don't hesitate to reach out for support when needed. Connecting with other homeschooling families, seeking advice from professionals, or joining support groups can provide valuable insights and encouragement. A strong network can make a significant difference, offering both practical help and emotional support.

8. **Embrace Flexibility:** One of the greatest advantages of

homeschooling is the flexibility it offers. Embrace this flexibility to create a learning environment that best suits your child's needs and interests. If something isn't working, don't be afraid to change course. Your ability to adapt is one of the most powerful tools you have as a homeschool educator.

9. **Celebrate Individuality**: Celebrate your child's individuality and unique learning style. Neurodivergent children often have remarkable strengths and talents that can flourish in the right environment. Focus on these strengths, and create opportunities for your child to shine in their own way.

By blending these practical strategies with a mindset of encouragement and support, you can build a homeschooling experience that is both effective and deeply rewarding. As you continue this journey, remember that growth and learning are ongoing processes—for both you and your child. Embrace the challenges, celebrate the successes, and trust in your ability to guide your child toward a bright and fulfilling future.

FINAL THOUGHTS

Homeschooling a neurodivergent child is a journey filled with both challenges and immense rewards. Throughout this book, we have explored the foundational elements necessary to create a successful homeschooling experience, from building a strong educational base to implementing visual learning strategies across subjects like mathematics, science, and the humanities. We have also discussed the importance of supporting your role as a parent-educator and finding a community that uplifts and guides you. Now, as you continue on this path, it's important to reflect on these core principles and carry them forward in your journey.

Every step of the homeschooling journey is an opportunity for growth, both for you and your child. From the foundational work of understanding your child's unique learning style to exploring various visual learning methods that make abstract concepts more tangible, each moment is a chance to deepen your connection and enhance your child's education. Embrace this journey with all its ups and downs,

186

knowing that your dedication is making a profound impact on your child's life.

Homeschooling requires resilience and a positive mindset. Whether you're navigating the challenges of adapting math lessons to suit visual learners, exploring creative ways to teach science through hands-on experiences, or integrating history and literature into a cohesive humanities curriculum, challenges will inevitably arise. However, with determination, flexibility, and the support of a strong community, you can overcome these obstacles and continue moving forward. Remember that every challenge is an opportunity to learn and grow, both as an educator and as a parent.

One of the greatest gifts you can give your child is a love of learning that extends beyond the confines of homeschooling. By incorporating visual learning strategies that make subjects like math, science, and the humanities more engaging, you are instilling in your child a sense of curiosity, critical thinking, and a passion for discovery. These are skills that will serve them throughout their life, far beyond their homeschooling years. Encourage your child to ask questions, explore new ideas, and see learning as a lifelong adventure.

As a parent-educator, your role is crucial to your child's success. You are not just teaching academic subjects; you are nurturing a safe, supportive environment where your child can thrive. Whether it's through the use of visual learning tools, the creation of a positive learning space, or the establishment of a strong support network, your efforts are laying the groundwork for your child's future success. Recognize and celebrate the love, dedication, and hard work you bring to this role every day.

As you reflect on your homeschooling journey, take pride in the progress you and your child have made. From the early days of uncertainty to the confidence you have built through experience, you have navigated this path with dedication, care, and a deep commitment to your child's well-being. The foundation you have established—grounded in visual learning strategies, supported by a strong community, and driven by continuous improvement—will continue to support you and your child as you move forward.

* * *

Trust in your abilities as an educator, seek out the support and resources you need, and embrace the journey ahead with an open heart and mind. With the tools and strategies you've developed, you and your child are well-equipped to thrive in your homeschooling experience, turning challenges into opportunities and creating a rich, fulfilling educational journey that will benefit your child for years to come.

CHAPTER ELEVEN

Resources for Visual Learning

BOOKS

When it comes to building a library that supports both learners and their guides, I'm a big fan of finding gently used books at a discount. Better World Books (www.betterworldbooks.org) is a favorite resource of mine, where you can often find barely used or inexpensive library-bound versions for extra durability—a must for those well-loved favorites! This list just touches on some of my personal favorite resources out there for homeschooling neurodivergent learners.

For the Learners:

Science:
- **The Science Ninjas Series** by Nathan Schreiber
  - Nathan Schreiber masterfully illustrates complex physics and chemistry topics through the adventures of genetically engineered super-humans in this graphic novel series. The stories are entertaining, accurate, and engaging, making physics and materials science not just accessible, but fun. These books have become a go-to for my child, even being packed for vacations! ((https://www.scienceninjas.com)

History:

- **The Good Times Travel Agency Series** by Linda Bailey and Bill Slavin
  - Adventures in the Ice Age is just one of the captivating titles in this series that combines adventure with historical education. Join the Binkertons—twins Josh and Emma, and their little sister Libby—as they embark on time-traveling journeys through history with the Vikings, Medieval Europe, Ancient China, Greece and Egypt. In Adventures in the Ice Age, the siblings find themselves deep-frozen in a prehistoric world, where they learn about the challenges and daily life of Early Modern Humans. The book mixes adventure with historical facts, making it an engaging way for children to learn about the past. The series is a fantastic blend of storytelling and educational content, ideal for young readers who love to explore history through imaginative adventures in a graphic novel format.
- **You Wouldn't Want to Be...** Series by Various Authors
  - This historical series brings the past to life with humorous, yet educational, narratives. Each book places the reader in the shoes of someone living through significant historical events, complete with quirky illustrations. This is a great way to engage learners who may find traditional history lessons dry or overwhelming.

Math:
- Avoid Hard Work!: ...And Other Encouraging Problem-Solving Tips for the Young, the Very Young, and the Young at Heart by Maria Droujkova, James Tanton, Yelena McManaman
  - This book encourages creative problem-solving and a playful approach to learning math. It's perfect for young learners and those who are young at heart, offering practical tips and a mindset that makes math feel more like a game than a chore. With 98 pages of engaging content, it's a great addition to any learner's library, especially those who might feel intimidated by traditional math approaches.
- **Math Adventures with Python** by Peter Farrell

- While this book is a bit more advanced, it offers a fantastic way for older learners interested in both math and programming to combine those passions. Using Python, learners can explore mathematical concepts by writing simple programs, making abstract math ideas like fractals, probability, and algebra more concrete and fun.

Mindfulness and Emotional Regulation:
- Mindful Kids Workbooks Series
  - The Mindful Kids workbooks offer an invaluable resource for children dealing with a range of emotions, including anxiety, grief, fear, sadness, anger, or experiences of bullying. These workbooks are designed to help learners process and work through difficult emotions using mindfulness techniques, creative activities, and reflective exercises. Each workbook is tailored to address specific feelings, providing tools that empower children to manage their emotions in healthy ways. Whether your child is coping with loss, facing challenges at school, or simply navigating the ups and downs of daily life, these workbooks offer practical, age-appropriate strategies to build emotional resilience. They are an excellent addition to any learner's library, helping to foster both emotional well-being and personal growth. (https://justoffnormal.com/search?q=mindful+kids)

For The Guides:

- **Visual Learning and Teaching: An Essential Guide for Educators K-8** by Susan Daniels
  - This book provides practical strategies and tools for implementing visual learning in the classroom. It's a must-read for educators who want to integrate more visual methods into their teaching, especially for neurodivergent learners.

- **The Big Picture: Rethinking Dyslexia** by James Redford and

Dylan Redford
- This book offers valuable insights into dyslexia and visual learning strategies. It's a great resource for understanding how visual tools can be used to support learners with dyslexia.

- **The Out-of-Sync Child Series** by Carol Stock Kranowitz
  - This series, including the third edition of The Out-of-Sync Child: Recognizing and Coping with Sensory Processing Differences, is an essential resource for parents and educators working with children who have sensory processing differences. Carol Stock Kranowitz provides practical strategies for recognizing and managing sensory challenges, making it easier to create supportive learning environments. The series also explores the evolving understanding of sensory processing, with additional titles like The Out-of-Sync Child Has Fun, which focuses on activities to help develop sensory integration. These books are comprehensive guides that are particularly valuable for those looking to better support neurodivergent learners in both educational and everyday settings.

- **The Dyslexia Empowerment Plan** by Ben Foss
  - Ben Foss provides a comprehensive approach to understanding and supporting dyslexic learners, including practical visual strategies. This is an empowering read for parents and educators alike.

- How Can I Talk If My Lips Don't Move?: Inside My Autistic Mind by Tito Rajarshi Mukhopadhyay
  - This autobiographical book offers a profound insight into the mind of a non-verbal autistic individual. It's an eye-opening resource for anyone looking to understand autism from an internal perspective, emphasizing the importance of presuming competence and finding alternative ways to communicate and learn.

- **Ido in Autismland: Climbing Out of Autism's Silent Prison** by Ido Kedar

- Ido Kedar shares his experiences as a non-verbal autistic person breaking out of the limitations imposed by others. This book is a powerful reminder of the need for patience, understanding, and the belief that every child can communicate and learn, even if they do so in non-traditional ways.

- Using Graphic Novels in the Science, Technology, Engineering, and Mathematics (STEM) Classroom by William Boerman-Cornell, David Klanderman, Sarah Klanderman

  - This book is a valuable resource for STEM educators who want to incorporate graphic novels into their teaching to engage students, explain difficult concepts, and enrich learning. The authors draw upon the latest educational research and decades of teaching experience to provide practical guidance for using graphic novels in the classroom. Each section of the book is dedicated to one element of STEM—Science, Technology, Engineering, and Mathematics—offering detailed strategies for how graphic novels can enhance instruction in each area. An appendix provides nearly 100 short reviews of graphic novels organized by topic, such as cryptography, evolution, computer coding, nuclear physics, and human physiology. This book is especially useful for educators seeking to make complex STEM subjects more accessible and engaging through the use of visual storytelling.

WEBSITES

In this section, you'll find a curated list of websites that offer a wide range of resources to support homeschooling, especially for neurodivergent learners. These sites provide everything from interactive learning tools and visual aids to comprehensive curriculum materials across various subjects like math, science, and the humanities. Whether you're looking for hands-on science experiments, digital flashcards, or innovative teaching strategies, these websites are invaluable resources for creating an engaging and personalized learning experience for your child.

Visit your local library and ask your librarian for additional resources. Many libraries host subscriptions to several educational resources that may include access to full curriculums, education games, live virtual field trips to the space station, the Alaskan tundra, or on-location visits related to US and World history

JustOffNormal.com

Visit my personal site for daily planners with goal tracking sheets, visual learning tools, curated math manipulatives like multiplication, subtraction, and fraction wrap-ups, hands-on STEM projects, social-emotional learning workbooks to support your learner's mental health and support for guides too.

General Educational Websites
- Khan Academy
  - Offers a wide range of free, visually rich educational videos and exercises in math, science, and more.
  - Website: www.khanacademy.org
- Edutopia
  - Features articles and resources on innovative teaching strategies, including visual learning techniques and social-emotional learning resources.
  - Website: www.edutopia.org
- MindMeister
  - An online mind mapping tool that helps create visual diagrams to organize thoughts and information.
  - Website: https://www.mindmeister.com
- Quizlet
  - A digital study tool that uses flashcards and visual aids to help students learn and retain information.
  - Website: https://quizlet.com
- Scratch
  - A visual programming language designed for easy use, allowing learners to create interactive stories, games, and animations.
  - Website: https://scratch.mit.edu
- Barefoot University

- Offers weekly forest school activities and nature exploration that teach nature-based sciences and outdoor skills, along with art, citizenship, local history, math, science, and more. Communities also engage in field trips and community service projects.
- Website: https://barefootuniversity.org

Math Web Resources

- Exploding Dots
  - A revolutionary technique that visually demonstrates mathematics from basic addition and subtraction to advanced concepts.
  - Website: https://globalmathproject.org/exploding-dots/
  - Additional Resources:
    - Friendly middle-school set of videos and workbook: (YouTube Playlist) and Downloadable Workbook
  - College Algebra course notes for high-school and university levels: Chapters 4, 7, 8
  - Engaging and understandable fractions: Chapters 5 and 6
  - Guzinta Math
    - Provides complete grade-level courses for grades 6-8 through browser extensions and web applets, utilizing the concepts behind Exploding Dots.
    - Website: https://guzintamath.com
- Math Playground
  - Features a wide variety of math games, puzzles, and interactive activities that make math fun and visually engaging. Topics range from basic arithmetic to more advanced concepts.
  - Website: https://www.mathplayground.com
- Prodigy Math Game
  - Combines math practice with a fantasy adventure game, making learning math engaging and immersive. It adapts to each learner's skill level, ensuring they are appropriately challenged.

- Website: https://www.prodigygame.com
- Coolmath4Kids
  - Offers fun math games, puzzles, and interactive lessons designed to make math enjoyable for kids. The colorful, playful interface is appealing to neurodiverse learners.
  - Website: https://www.coolmath4kids.com
- Math Antics
  - Provides free instructional videos that break down math concepts with clear visuals and easy-to-understand explanations. The videos are engaging and make learning math concepts more accessible.
  - Website: https://www.mathantics.com
- Numberphile
  - A YouTube channel dedicated to visually exploring interesting mathematical concepts and problems. The content ranges from basic to advanced topics, presented in a way that is visually stimulating and thought-provoking.
  - Website: https://www.youtube.com/user/numberphile
- GeoGebra
  - A dynamic mathematics software that brings together geometry, algebra, spreadsheets, graphing, statistics, and calculus in an interactive and visual way. It's great for learners who benefit from hands-on visual learning.
  - Website: https://www.geogebra.org
- DragonBox
  - An award-winning series of educational math games that teach key math concepts through engaging gameplay. The visuals and interactive elements make it especially suitable for neurodiverse learners.
  - Website: https://dragonbox.com
- Desmos
  - A powerful graphing calculator and interactive math tool that allows learners to visualize equations and concepts. It's particularly useful for exploring algebra, calculus, and other advanced math topics visually.
  - Website: https://www.desmos.com

- Science Mom and Math Dad
  - Provides a range of math and science courses that incorporate visual learning techniques, hands-on experiments, and real-world applications to make science concepts accessible and engaging. Designed with neurodiverse learners in mind, these courses inspire curiosity and foster a deeper understanding of the natural world. Courses are held live and asynchronous, pre-recorded versions are also available. Aimed at the middle-school ages but can be adapted for younger or extended for the more curious. Science Mom's background in molecular biology and Math Dad's PhD in Mathematics help to bring depth to topics with loads of fun dad jokes, music, and hand-illustrated workbooks with lots of comic style elements to keep your learner engaged.
  - Website: https://www.science.mom

Humanities Web Resources
- ReadWriteThink Story Map
  - An interactive tool for secondary students studying literary or historical events. It includes graphic organizers to facilitate both pre-reading and post-writing activities, helping students map out key elements of character, setting, conflict, and resolution.
  - Website: https://www.readwritethink.org/classroom-resources/student-interactives/drama
- ReadWriteThink Trading Card Creator
  - A creative tool that allows students to demonstrate their literacy knowledge by creating trading cards about real or fictional people, places, events, or abstract concepts. It's an excellent prewriting exercise that encourages critical thinking and personal connections.
  - Website: https://www.readwritethink.org/classroom-resources/student-interactives/trading-card-creator
- Money Prep
  - Free games for teaching financial literacy to students.
  - Website: https://www.moneyprep.com

- iCivics
  - Provides game-based interactive lessons on civics topics, including government branches, citizenship, elections, voting, and more.
  - Website: https://vision.icivics.org

Science Web Resources
- NASA: Games and Interactives
  - A collection of engaging games and interactive resources that explore various scientific concepts and space missions.
  - Website: https://www.nasa.gov/interactives
- CK-12 Foundation
  - Provides free textbooks and interactive visual simulations for a variety of subjects, offering customizable learning experiences for students.
  - Website: https://www.ck12.org
- Printables (3D Models)
  - Offers resources for 3D printing models, which can be sent to your local library's 3D printer. A useful tool for hands-on models, such as a Balloon Powered Radial Engine.
  - Website: https://www.printables.com
- Supercharged Science
  - An online or DVD-based hands-on science curriculum program packed with experiments taught by engineers and scientists, covering physics, chemistry, life science, biology, and earth science for K-12.
  - Website: https://www.sciencelearningspace2.com
- Origami Organelles
  - Offers printable 3D paper models covering biology, chemistry, earth science, and physics.
  - Website: https://origamiorganelles.com
- Science Mom and Math Dad
  - Provides a range of math and science courses that incorporate visual learning techniques, hands-on experiments, and real-world applications to make science concepts accessible and engaging. Designed with neurodiverse learners in mind, these courses

inspire curiosity and foster a deeper understanding of the natural world. Science Mom's background in molecular biology and plant science and Math Dad's PhD in Mathematics help to bring depth to topics with loads of fun dad jokes, music, and hand-illustrated workbooks with lots of comic style elements to keep your learner engaged.
- Website: https://www.science.mom

Virtual Field Trips
- Discovery Education
  - Provides a variety of virtual field trips that cover topics ranging from natural disasters to space exploration.
  - Website: https://www.discoveryeducation.com/community/virtual-field-trips
- Google Arts & Culture
  - Explore museums, historical sites, and cultural landmarks from around the world through interactive tours and exhibits.
  - Website: https://artsandculture.google.com
- Smithsonian National Museum of Natural History
  - Offers virtual tours of their exhibits, allowing learners to explore natural history collections from anywhere.
  - Website: https://naturalhistory.si.edu/visit/virtual-tour
- NASA Virtual Field Trips
  - Offers a range of virtual tours and interactive experiences related to space exploration and science.
  - Website: https://www.nasa.gov/
- The Nature Conservancy Virtual Field Trips
  - Explore ecosystems, wildlife, and conservation efforts around the world through interactive online experiences.
  - Website: https://www.nature.org/en-us/get-involved/how-to-help/places-we-protect/virtual-field-trips/
- Monterey Bay Aquarium Live Cams
  - Provides live streaming of various aquarium exhibits, allowing learners to observe marine life in real-time.

- Website: https://www.montereybayaquarium.org/animals/live-cams
- Ellis Island Virtual Tour
  - Offers an interactive tour of Ellis Island, exploring the history of immigration in the United States.
  - Website: https://www.nps.gov/hdp/exhibits/ellis/Ellis_Index.html
- National Geographic Kids Virtual Field Trips
  - Features a variety of virtual field trips on topics like wildlife, geography, and history, designed for younger learners.
  - Website: https://kids.nationalgeographic.com/videos/virtual-field-trip/
- Great Wall of China Virtual Tour
  - Explore the ancient Great Wall of China through an immersive virtual experience that provides historical context and stunning visuals.
  - Website: https://www.thechinaguide.com/destination/great-wall-of-china
- Yellowstone National Park Virtual Tours
  - Offers virtual tours of Yellowstone's famous landmarks, including geysers, hot springs, and wildlife.
  - Website: https://www.nps.gov/yell/learn/photosmultimedia/virtualtours.htm

Virtual Reality

These resources use a simple adaptor for your cell phone like Google Cardboard for immersive lessons that dive into cell biology to take you on history expeditions.

- Google Expeditions
  - Offers a vast library of virtual field trips and immersive experiences across various subjects, including science, history, and geography.
  - Website: https://edu.google.com/products/vr-ar/expeditions/
- Discovery VR
  - Provides engaging virtual reality experiences from the Discovery Channel, covering topics like nature, space, and history.

- Website: https://www.discoveryvr.com/
- Unimersiv
  - Offers educational VR experiences in topics such as anatomy, history, and space exploration, making learning immersive and interactive.
  - Website: http://unimersiv.com/
- Nearpod VR
  - Integrates VR lessons into its interactive learning platform, covering a wide range of educational topics, including science, social studies, and more.
  - Website: https://nearpod.com/vr
- InMind VR
  - A neuroscience-based educational game that takes users on a journey through the human brain to learn about neurons and brain chemistry.
  - Website: https://inmind-vr.com/
- Titans of Space
  - Provides a VR tour of the solar system, allowing learners to explore planets, moons, and other celestial bodies in a detailed and immersive way.
  - Website: http://www.titansofspacevr.com/
- Lifeliqe VR Museum
  - Features interactive 3D models and simulations of various scientific topics, including biology, chemistry, and physics, in an engaging VR format.
  - Website: https://www.lifeliqe.com/vr
- Anatomyou VR
  - Provides an immersive tour inside the human body, helping learners explore various systems like the circulatory and respiratory systems in detail.
  - Website: https://anatomyou.com/
- VR Gorilla
  - Offers a variety of 360-degree videos on nature, wildlife, and environmental topics, providing immersive virtual experiences.
  - Website: https://www.vr-gorilla.com/
- Cospaces Edu
  - Allows users to create and explore their own virtual reality experiences, combining coding, creativity, and educational content for a personalized learning

experience.
- Website: https://cospaces.io/edu/